MznLnx

Missing Links Exam Preps

Exam Prep for

Finite Mathematics

Rolf, 6th Edition

The MznLnx Exam Prep is your link from the texbook and lecture to your exams.
The MznLnx Exam Preps are unauthorized and comprehensive reviews of your textbooks.

All material provided by MznLnx and Rico Publications (c) 2010
Textbook publishers and textbook authors do not particpate in or contribute to these reviews.

MznLnx

Rico
Publications

Exam Prep for Finite Mathematics
6th Edition
Rolf

Publisher: Raymond Houge
Assistant Editor: Michael Rouger
Text and Cover Designer: Lisa Buckner
Marketing Manager: Sara Swagger
Project Manager, Editorial Production: Jerry Emerson
Art Director: Vernon Lowerui

Product Manager: Dave Mason
Editorial Assitant: Rachel Guzmanji
Pedagogy: Debra Long
Cover Image: Jim Reed/Getty Images
Text and Cover Printer: City Printing, Inc.
Compositor: Media Mix, Inc.

(c) 2010 Rico Publications

ALL RIGHTS RESERVED. No part of this work covered by the copyright may be reproduced or used in any form or by an means--graphic, electronic, or mechanical, including photocopying, recording, taping, Web distribution, information storage, and retrieval systems, or in any other manner--without the written permission of the publisher.

For more information about our products, contact us at:
Dave.Mason@RicoPublications.com

For permission to use material from this text or product, submit a request online to:
Dave.Mason@RicoPublications.com

Printed in the United States
ISBN:

Contents

CHAPTER 1
FUNCTIONS AND LINES 1

CHAPTER 2
LINEAR SYSTEMS 8

CHAPTER 3
LINEAR PROGRAMMING 22

CHAPTER 4
LINEAR PROGRAMMING: THE SIMPLEX METHOD 28

CHAPTER 5
MATHEMATICS Of FINANCE 35

CHAPTER 6
SETS AND COUNTING 39

CHAPTER 7
PROBABILITY 49

CHAPTER 8
STATISTICS 58

CHAPTER 9
GAME THEORY 76

CHAPTER 10
LOGIC 78

ANSWER KEY 86

TO THE STUDENT

COMPREHENSIVE

The *MznLnx* Exam Prep series is designed to help you pass your exams. Editors at MznLnx review your textbooks and then prepare these practice exams to help you master the textbook material. Unlike study guides, workbooks, and practice tests provided by the texbook publisher and textbook authors, *MznLnx* gives you **all** of the material in each chapter in exam form, not just samples, so you can be sure to nail your exam.

MECHANICAL

The MznLnx Exam Prep series creates exams that will help you learn the subject matter as well as test you on your understanding. Each question is designed to help you master the concept. Just working through the exams, you gain an understanding of the subject--its a simple mechanical process that produces success.

INTEGRATED STUDY GUIDE AND REVIEW

MznLnx is not just a set of exams designed to test you, its also a comprehensive review of the subject content. Each exam question is also a review of the concept, making sure that you will get the answer correct without having to go to other sources of material. You learn as you go! Its the easiest way to pass an exam.

HUMOR

Studying can be tedious and dry. MznLnx's instructional design includes moderate humor within the exam questions on occassion, to break the tedium and revitalize the brain

Chapter 1. FUNCTIONS AND LINES

1. _____ and independent variables refer to values that change in relationship to each other. The _____ are those that are observed to change in response to the independent variables. The independent variables are those that are deliberately manipulated to invoke a change in the _____.
    a. Dependent variables
    b. Steiner system
    c. Yates analysis
    d. Round robin test

2. In mathematics, especially in the area of abstract algebra known as ring theory, a _____ is a ring with 0 ≠ 1 such that ab = 0 implies that either a = 0 or b = 0. That is, it is a nontrivial ring without left or right zero divisors. A commutative _____ is called an integral _____.
    a. Simple ring
    b. Left primitive ring
    c. Domain
    d. Modular representation theory

3. The mathematical concept of a _____ expresses the intuitive idea of deterministic dependence between two quantities, one of which is viewed as primary and the other as secondary. A _____ then is a way to associate a unique output for each input of a specified type, for example, a real number or an element of a given set.
    a. Going up
    b. Coherent
    c. Function
    d. Grill

4. Dependent variables and _____ refer to values that change in relationship to each other. The dependent variables are those that are observed to change in response to the _____. The _____ are those that are deliberately manipulated to invoke a change in the dependent variables.
    a. Operational confound
    b. Experimental design diagram
    c. One-factor-at-a-time method
    d. Independent variables

5. In descriptive statistics, the _____ is the length of the smallest interval which contains all the data. It is calculated by subtracting the smallest observations from the greatest and provides an indication of statistical dispersion.

It is measured in the same units as the data.

a. Range
b. Class
c. Kernel
d. Bandwidth

6. In mathematics, an _____ is a statement about the relative size or order of two objects, or about whether they are the same or not

- The notation a < b means that a is less than b.
- The notation a > b means that a is greater than b.
- The notation a ≠ b means that a is not equal to b, but does not say that one is bigger than the other or even that they can be compared in size.

In all these cases, a is not equal to b, hence, '_____'.

These relations are known as strict _____

- The notation a ≤ b means that a is less than or equal to b;
- The notation a ≥ b means that a is greater than or equal to b;

An additional use of the notation is to show that one quantity is much greater than another, normally by several orders of magnitude.

- The notation a << b means that a is much less than b.
- The notation a >> b means that a is much greater than b.

If the sense of the _____ is the same for all values of the variables for which its members are defined, then the _____ is called an 'absolute' or 'unconditional' _____. If the sense of an _____ holds only for certain values of the variables involved, but is reversed or destroyed for other values of the variables, it is called a conditional _____.

An _____ may appear unsolvable because it only states whether a number is larger or smaller than another number; but it is possible to apply the same operations for equalities to inequalities. For example, to find x for the _____ 10x > 23 one would divide 23 by 10.

a. A Mathematical Theory of Communication
b. A chemical equation
c. A posteriori
d. Inequality

7. In mathematics a _____ is an inequality which involves a linear function.

Chapter 1. FUNCTIONS AND LINES

When operating in terms of real numbers, linear inequalities are the ones written in the forms

$$f(x) < b \text{ or } f(x) \leq b,$$

where f(x) is a linear functional in real numbers and b is a constant real number. Alternatively, these may be viewed as

$$g(x) < 0 \text{ or } g(x) \leq 0,$$

where g(x) is an affine function.

a. Levi-Civita symbol
b. Split-complex number
c. Generalized singular value decomposition
d. Linear inequality

8. _____ is used to describe the steepness, incline, gradient, or grade of a straight line. A higher _____ value indicates a steeper incline. The _____ is defined as the ratio of the 'rise' divided by the 'run' between two points on a line, or in other words, the ratio of the altitude change to the horizontal distance between any two points on the line.

a. Cognitively Guided Instruction
b. Number line
c. Point plotting
d. Slope

9. The _____ of any solid, plasma, vacuum or theoretical object is how much three-dimensional space it occupies, often quantified numerically. One-dimensional figures and two-dimensional shapes are assigned zero _____ in the three-dimensional space. _____ is presented as ml or cm^3.

_____s of straight-edged and circular shapes are calculated using arithmetic formulae.

a. Thermodynamic limit
b. Cauchy momentum equation
c. Stress-energy tensor
d. Volume

10. In mathematics and in the sciences, a _____ (plural: _____e, formulæ or _____s) is a concise way of expressing information symbolically (as in a mathematical or chemical _____), or a general relationship between quantities. One of many famous _____e is Albert Einstein's E = mc^2 (see special relativity

Chapter 1. FUNCTIONS AND LINES

In mathematics, a _____ is a key to solve an equation with variables. For example, the problem of determining the volume of a sphere is one that requires a significant amount of integral calculus to solve.

a. 120-cell
b. 2-3 heap
c. 1-center problem
d. Formula

11. In mathematics, a _____ is a function whose values do not vary and thus are constant. For example, if we have the function f→ B is a _____ if f
a. Linear operator
b. Squeeze mapping
c. Constant function
d. Point reflection

12. In mathematics, a _____ is a rectangular table of elements, which may be numbers or, more generally, any abstract quantities that can be added and multiplied. Matrices are used to describe linear equations, keep track of the coefficients of linear transformations and to record data that depend on multiple parameters. Matrices are described by the field of _____ theory.
a. Compression
b. Coherent
c. Double counting
d. Matrix

13. In mathematics, the _____ is an approach to finding a particular solution to certain inhomogeneous ordinary differential equations and recurrence relations. It is closely related to the annihilator method, but instead of using a particular kind of differential operator in order to find the best possible form of the particular solution, a 'guess' is made as to the appropriate form, which is then tested by differentiating the resulting equation. In this sense, the _____ is less formal but more intuitive than the annihilator method.
a. Phase line
b. Differential algebraic equations
c. Linear differential equation
d. Method of undetermined coefficients

14. In mathematics, the _____ of a number n is the number that, when added to n, yields zero. The _____ of n is denoted −n. For example, 7 is −7, because 7 + (−7) = 0, and the _____ of −0.3 is 0.3, because −0.3 + 0.3 = 0.

a. Arity
b. Algebraic structure
c. Additive inverse
d. Associativity

15. A _____ of a curve is the envelope of a family of congruent circles centered on the curve. It generalises the concept of _____ lines.

It is sometimes called the offset curve but the term 'offset' often refers also to translation.

a. Cycloid
b. Bifolium
c. Cissoid
d. Parallel

16. The existence and properties of _____ are the basis of Euclid's parallel postulate. _____ are two lines on the same plane that do not intersect even assuming that lines extend to infinity in either direction.

a. Parallel lines
b. Vertical translation
c. Spidron
d. Square wheel

17. A _____ is an abstract model that uses mathematical language to describe the behavior of a system. Eykhoff defined a _____ as 'a representation of the essential aspects of an existing system which presents knowledge of that system in usable form'.

a. Metaheuristic
b. Rata Die
c. Total least squares
d. Mathematical model

18. In economics, business, retail, and accounting, a _____ is the value of money that has been used up to produce something, and hence is not available for use anymore. In business, the _____ may be one of acquisition, in which case the amount of money expended to acquire it is counted as _____. In this case, money is the input that is gone in order to acquire the thing.

a. 1-center problem
b. 120-cell
c. Cost
d. 2-3 heap

19. In economics, specifically cost accounting, the _____ is the point at which cost or expenses and revenue are equal: there is no net loss or gain, and one has 'broken even'. Therefore has not made a profit or a loss.

In the linear Cost-Volume-Profit Analysis model, the _____ can be directly computed in terms of Total Revenue and Total Costs as:

$$TR = TC$$
$$P \times X = TFC + V \times X$$
$$P \times X - V \times X = TFC$$
$$(P - V) \times X = TFC$$
$$X = \frac{TFC}{P - V}$$

where:

- TFC is Total Fixed Costs,
- P is Unit Sale Price, and
- V is Unit Variable Cost.

The _____ can alternatively be computed as the point where Contribution equals Fixed Costs.

The quantity $(P - V)$ is of interest in its own right, and is called the Unit Contribution Margin: it is the marginal profit per unit, or alternatively the portion of each sale that contributes to Fixed Costs. Thus the _____ can be more simply computed as the point where Total Contribution = Total Fixed Cost:

$$\text{Total Contribution} = \text{Total Fixed Costs}$$
$$\text{Unit Contribution} \times \text{Number of Units} = \text{Total Fixed Costs}$$
$$\text{Number of Units} = \frac{\text{Total Fixed Costs}}{\text{Unit Contribution}}$$

In currency units to reach break-even, one can use the above calculation and multiply by Price, or equivalently use the

$$\text{Break-even(in Sales)} = \frac{\text{Fixed Costs}}{C/P}.$$

Contribution Margin Ratio to compute it as:

R=C Where R is revenue generated C is cost incurred.

a. 120-cell
b. 1-center problem
c. Small numbers game
d. Break-even point

20. In accounting, _____ or carrying value is the value of an asset or according to its balance sheet account balance. For assets, the value is based on the original cost of the asset less any depreciation, amortization or impairment costs made against the asset. A company's _____ is its total assets minus intangible assets and liabilities.

a. 120-cell
b. 1-center problem
c. Depreciation
d. Book value

21. _____ is a term used in accounting, economics and finance to spread the cost of an asset over the span of several years.

In simple words we can say that _____ is the reduction in the value of an asset due to usage, passage of time, wear and tear, technological outdating or obsolescence, depletion or other such factors.

In accounting, _____ is a term used to describe any method of attributing the historical or purchase cost of an asset across its useful life, roughly corresponding to normal wear and tear.

a. Gross sales
b. Depreciation
c. 120-cell
d. 1-center problem

Chapter 2. LINEAR SYSTEMS

1. In linear algebra, _____ is a version of Gaussian elimination that puts zeros both above and below each pivot element as it goes from the top row of the given matrix to the bottom. In other words, _____ brings a matrix to reduced row echelon form, whereas Gaussian elimination takes it only as far as row echelon form. Every matrix has a reduced row echelon form, and this algorithm is guaranteed to produce it.

   a. Conservation form
   b. Gauss-Jordan elimination
   c. Spheroidal wave functions
   d. Lax equivalence theorem

2. In mathematics, an _____ is a statement about the relative size or order of two objects, or about whether they are the same or not

   - The notation a < b means that a is less than b.
   - The notation a > b means that a is greater than b.
   - The notation a ≠ b means that a is not equal to b, but does not say that one is bigger than the other or even that they can be compared in size.

   In all these cases, a is not equal to b, hence, '_____'.

   These relations are known as strict _____

   - The notation a ≤ b means that a is less than or equal to b;
   - The notation a ≥ b means that a is greater than or equal to b;

   An additional use of the notation is to show that one quantity is much greater than another, normally by several orders of magnitude.

   - The notation a << b means that a is much less than b.
   - The notation a >> b means that a is much greater than b.

   If the sense of the _____ is the same for all values of the variables for which its members are defined, then the _____ is called an 'absolute' or 'unconditional' _____. If the sense of an _____ holds only for certain values of the variables involved, but is reversed or destroyed for other values of the variables, it is called a conditional _____.

   An _____ may appear unsolvable because it only states whether a number is larger or smaller than another number; but it is possible to apply the same operations for equalities to inequalities. For example, to find x for the _____ 10x > 23 one would divide 23 by 10.

Chapter 2. LINEAR SYSTEMS

a. A Mathematical Theory of Communication
b. A posteriori
c. A chemical equation
d. Inequality

3. In mathematics a _____ is an inequality which involves a linear function.

When operating in terms of real numbers, linear inequalities are the ones written in the forms

$$f(x) < b \text{ or } f(x) \leq b,$$

where f(x) is a linear functional in real numbers and b is a constant real number. Alternatively, these may be viewed as

$$g(x) < 0 \text{ or } g(x) \leq 0,$$

where g(x) is an affine function.

a. Split-complex number
b. Linear inequality
c. Generalized singular value decomposition
d. Levi-Civita symbol

4. In the study of metric spaces in mathematics, there are various notions of two metrics on the same underlying space being 'the same', or _____.

In the following, M will denote a non-empty set and d_1 and d_2 will denote two metrics on M.

The two metrics d_1 and d_2 are said to be topologically _____ if they generate the same topology on M.

a. A chemical equation
b. A Mathematical Theory of Communication
c. A posteriori
d. Equivalent

Chapter 2. LINEAR SYSTEMS

5. _____ is an economic model describing effects on price and quantity in a market. It predicts that in a competitive market, price will function to equalize the quantity demanded by consumers, and the quantity supplied by producers, resulting in an economic equilibrium of price and quantity. The model incorporates other factors changing equilibrium as a shift of demand and/or supply.
   a. 1-center problem
   b. Supply and demand
   c. Cross price elasticity of demand
   d. Marginal rate of substitution

6. In mathematics, a _____ is, informally, an infinitely vast and infinitely thin sheet. _____s may be thought of as objects in some higher dimensional space, or they may be considered without any outside space, as in the setting of Euclidean geometry
   a. Blocking
   b. Bandwidth
   c. Plane
   d. Group

7. In mathematics, _____ are two-dimensional manifolds or surfaces that are perfectly flat.
   a. 120-cell
   b. 2-3 heap
   c. 1-center problem
   d. Planes

8. In mathematics, the _____ of two sets A and B is the set that contains all elements of A that also belong to B, but no other elements.

For explanation of the symbols used in this article, refer to the table of mathematical symbols.

The _____ of A and B

Chapter 2. LINEAR SYSTEMS

The _____ of A and B is written 'A ∩ B'. Formally:

x is an element of A ∩ B if and only if
- x is an element of A and
- x is an element of B.

For example:
- The _____ of the sets {1, 2, 3} and {2, 3, 4} is {2, 3}.
- The number 9 is not in the _____ of the set of prime numbers {2, 3, 5, 7, 11, â€¦} and the set of odd numbers {1, 3, 5, 7, 9, 11, â€¦}.

If the _____ of two sets A and B is empty, that is they have no elements in common, then they are said to be disjoint, denoted: A ∩ B = Ø. For example the sets {1, 2} and {3, 4} are disjoint, written {1, 2} ∩ {3, 4} = Ø.

a. Intersection
b. Advice
c. Erlang
d. Order

9. In linear algebra, a column vector or _____ is an m × 1 matrix, i.e. a matrix consisting of a single column of m elements.

$$\mathbf{x} = \begin{bmatrix} x_1 \\ x_2 \\ \vdots \\ x_m \end{bmatrix}$$

The transpose of a column vector is a row vector and vice versa.

The set of all column vectors forms a vector space which is the dual space to the set of all row vectors.

a. Split-complex number
b. Spread of a matrix
c. Cayley-Hamilton theorem
d. Column matrix

10. In mathematics, an _____ or member of a set is any one of the distinct objects that make up that set.

Writing A = {1,2,3,4}, means that the _____s of the set A are the numbers 1, 2, 3 and 4. Groups of _____s of A, for example {1,2}, are subsets of A.

a. Ideal
b. Universal code
c. Order
d. Element

11. In mathematics, a _____ is a rectangular table of elements, which may be numbers or, more generally, any abstract quantities that can be added and multiplied. Matrices are used to describe linear equations, keep track of the coefficients of linear transformations and to record data that depend on multiple parameters. Matrices are described by the field of _____ theory.
   a. Coherent
   b. Compression
   c. Matrix
   d. Double counting

12. In linear algebra, a row vector or _____ is a 1 × n matrix, that is, a matrix consisting of a single row:

$$\mathbf{x} = \begin{bmatrix} x_1 & x_2 & \ldots & x_m \end{bmatrix}.$$

The transpose of a row vector is a column vector:

$$\begin{bmatrix} x_1 \\ x_2 \\ \vdots \\ x_m \end{bmatrix} = \begin{bmatrix} x_1 & x_2 & \ldots & x_m \end{bmatrix}^{\mathrm{T}}.$$

The set of all row vectors forms a vector space which is the dual space to the set of all column vectors.

Chapter 2. LINEAR SYSTEMS

Row vectors are sometimes written using the following non-standard notation:

$$\mathbf{x} = \begin{bmatrix} x_1, x_2, \ldots, x_m \end{bmatrix}.$$

- Matrix multiplication involves the action of multiplying each row vector of one matrix by each column vector of another matrix.

- The dot product of two vectors a and b is equivalent to multiplying the row vector representation of a by the column vector representation of b:

$$\mathbf{a} \cdot \mathbf{b} = \begin{bmatrix} a_1 & a_2 & a_3 \end{bmatrix} \begin{bmatrix} b_1 \\ b_2 \\ b_3 \end{bmatrix}.$$

a. Dual vector space
b. Gram-Schmidt process
c. Woodbury matrix identity
d. Row matrix

13. In linear algebra, the _____ of a matrix is obtained by changing a matrix in some way.

Given the matrices A and B, where:

$$A = \begin{bmatrix} 1 & 3 & 2 \\ 2 & 0 & 1 \\ 5 & 2 & 2 \end{bmatrix}, \quad B = \begin{bmatrix} 4 \\ 3 \\ 1 \end{bmatrix}$$

Then, the _____ is written as:

$$(A|B) = \begin{bmatrix} 1 & 3 & 2 & 4 \\ 2 & 0 & 1 & 3 \\ 5 & 2 & 2 & 1 \end{bmatrix}$$

This is useful when solving systems of linear equations or the _____ may also be used to find the inverse of a matrix by combining it with the identity matrix.

Chapter 2. LINEAR SYSTEMS

Let C be a square 2×2 matrix where $C = \begin{bmatrix} 1 & 3 \\ -5 & 0 \end{bmatrix}$

To find the inverse of C we create where I is the 2×2 identity matrix.

a. Unimodular polynomial matrix
b. Alternating sign matrix
c. Eigendecomposition
d. Augmented matrix

14. In mathematics, a _____ is a constant multiplicative factor of a certain object. For example, in the expression $9x^2$, the _____ of x^2 is 9.

The object can be such things as a variable, a vector, a function, etc.

a. Stability radius
b. Multivariate division algorithm
c. Fibonacci polynomials
d. Coefficient

15. In mathematics, a _____ (or matrix element) is a function on a group of a special form, which depends on a linear representation of the group and additional data. For the case of a finite group, _____s express the action of the elements of the group in the specified representation via the entries of the corresponding matrices.

_____s of representations of Lie groups turned out to be intimately related with the theory of special functions, providing a unifying approach to large parts of this theory.

a. K-finite
b. Matrix coefficient
c. Springer representations
d. Regular representation

16. _____ is a branch of mathematics which focuses on the study of matrices. Initially a sub-branch of linear algebra, it has grown to cover subjects related to graph theory, algebra, combinatorics, and statistics as well.

The term matrix was first coined in 1848 by J.J. Sylvester as a name of an array of numbers.

Chapter 2. LINEAR SYSTEMS

a. Semi-simple operators
b. Pairing
c. Segre classification
d. Matrix theory

17. In the geometry of the projective plane, _____ refers to geometric transformations that replace points by lines and lines by points while preserving incidence properties among the transformed objects. The existence of such transformations leads to a general principle, that any theorem about incidences between points and lines in the projective plane may be transformed into another theorem about lines and points, by a substitution of the appropriate words.

_____ in the projective plane is a special case of _____ for projective spaces, transformations that interchange

dimension + codimension.

a. Decidable
b. Duality
c. Blocking
d. Disk

18. In linear algebra a matrix is in _____ if

- All nonzero rows are above any rows of all zeroes, and
- The leading coefficient of a row is always strictly to the right of the leading coefficient of the row above it.

This is the definition used in this article, but some texts add a third condition:

- The leading coefficient of each nonzero row is one.

A matrix is in reduced _____ if it satisfies the above three conditions, and if, in addition

- Every leading coefficient is the only nonzero entry in its column.

The first non-zero entry in each row is called a pivot.

This matrix is in reduced _____:

$$\begin{bmatrix} 0 & 1 & 4 & 0 & 0 \\ 0 & 0 & 0 & 1 & 0 \\ 0 & 0 & 0 & 0 & 1 \\ 0 & 0 & 0 & 0 & 0 \end{bmatrix}.$$

The following matrix is also in _____, but not in reduced row form:

$$\begin{bmatrix} 1 & 1 & 1 & 1 \\ 0 & 9 & 0 & 2 \\ 0 & 0 & 0 & 3 \end{bmatrix}.$$

However, this matrix is not in _____, as the leading coefficient of row 3 is not strictly to the right of the leading coefficient of row 2.

$$\begin{bmatrix} 1 & 2 & 3 & 4 \\ 0 & 3 & 7 & 2 \\ 0 & 2 & 0 & 0 \end{bmatrix}$$

Every non-zero matrix can be reduced to an infinite number of echelon forms via elementary matrix transformations.

a. Portable, Extensible Toolkit for Scientific Computation
b. Gaussian elimination
c. Reduced row echelon form
d. Row echelon form

19. In mathematics, _____ is one of the basic operations defining a vector space in linear algebra. Note that _____ is different from scalar product which is an inner product between two vectors.

More specifically, if K is a field and V is a vector space over K, then _____ is a function from K × V to V.

Chapter 2. LINEAR SYSTEMS

a. Non-negative matrix factorization
b. Jordan normal form
c. Frobenius normal form
d. Scalar multiplication

20. _____ is the mathematical operation of scaling one number by another. It is one of the four basic operations in elementary arithmetic.

_____ is defined for whole numbers in terms of repeated addition; for example, 4 multiplied by 3 can be calculated by adding 3 copies of 4 together:

$$4 + 4 + 4 = 12.$$

_____ of rational numbers and real numbers is defined by systematic generalization of this basic idea.

a. Multiplication
b. The number 0 is even.
c. Highest common factor
d. Least common multiple

21. In mathematics, the _____ is an operation which takes two vectors over the real numbers R and returns a real-valued scalar quantity. It is the standard inner product of the orthonormal Euclidean space.

The _____ of two vectors a = [a_1, a_2, …, a_n] and b = [b_1, b_2, …, b_n] is defined as:

$$\mathbf{a} \cdot \mathbf{b} = \sum_{i=1}^{n} a_i b_i = a_1 b_1 + a_2 b_2 + \cdots + a_n b_n$$

where Σ denotes summation notation and n is the dimension of the vectors.

a. Principal axis theorem
b. Conjugate transpose
c. Matrix determinant lemma
d. Dot product

22. In mathematics, _____ is the operation of multiplying a matrix with either a scalar or another matrix

This is the most often used and most important way to multiply matrices.

Chapter 2. LINEAR SYSTEMS

a. Matrix calculus
b. Logarithmic norm
c. Jordan matrix
d. Matrix multiplication

23. In mathematics, the term _____ has several different important meanings:

- An _____ is an equality that remains true regardless of the values of any variables that appear within it, to distinguish it from an equality which is true under more particular conditions. For this, the 'triple bar' symbol ≡ is sometimes used.
- In algebra, an _____ or _____ element of a set S with a binary operation Â· is an element e that, when combined with any element x of S, produces that same x. That is, eÂ·x = xÂ·e = x for all x in S.
    - The _____ function from a set S to itself, often denoted id or id_S, s the function such that i = x for all x in S. This function serves as the _____ element in the set of all functions from S to itself with respect to function composition.
    - In linear algebra, the _____ matrix of size n is the n-by-n square matrix with ones on the main diagonal and zeros elsewhere. This matrix serves as the _____ with respect to matrix multiplication.

A common example of the first meaning is the trigonometric _____

$$\sin^2 \theta + \cos^2 \theta = 1$$

which is true for all real values of θ, as opposed to

$$\cos \theta = 1,$$

which is true only for some values of θ, not all. For example, the latter equation is true when $\theta = 0$, false when $\theta = 2$

The concepts of 'additive _____' and 'multiplicative _____' are central to the Peano axioms. The number 0 is the 'additive _____' for integers, real numbers, and complex numbers. For the real numbers, for all $a \in \mathbb{R}$,

$$0 + a = a,$$

$$a + 0 = a, \text{ and}$$

$$0 + 0 = 0.$$

Similarly, The number 1 is the 'multiplicative _____' for integers, real numbers, and complex numbers.

a. Identity
b. Action
c. Intersection
d. ARIA

24. In linear algebra, the _____ or unit matrix of size n is the n-by-n square matrix with ones on the main diagonal and zeros elsewhere. It is denoted by I_n, or simply by I if the size is immaterial or can be trivially determined by the context. (In some fields, such as quantum mechanics, the _____ is denoted by a boldface one, 1; otherwise it is identical to I.)

a. Unital
b. Arity
c. Associativity
d. Identity matrix

25. In linear algebra, a _____ is a square matrix in which the entries outside the main diagonal are all zero. The diagonal entries themselves may or may not be zero. Thus, the matrix D = with n columns and n rows is diagonal if:

$$d_{i,j} = 0 \text{ if } i \neq j \quad \forall i,j \in \{1, 2, \ldots, n\}$$

For example, the following matrix is diagonal:

$$\begin{bmatrix} 1 & 0 & 0 \\ 0 & 4 & 0 \\ 0 & 0 & -3 \end{bmatrix}.$$

The term _____ may sometimes refer to a rectangular _____, which is an m-by-n matrix with only the entries of the form $d_{i,i}$ possibly non-zero; for example,

$$\begin{bmatrix} 1 & 0 & 0 \\ 0 & 4 & 0 \\ 0 & 0 & -3 \\ 0 & 0 & 0 \end{bmatrix}, \text{ or } \begin{bmatrix} 1 & 0 & 0 & 0 & 0 \\ 0 & 4 & 0 & 0 & 0 \\ 0 & 0 & -3 & 0 & 0 \end{bmatrix}.$$

a. Transition matrix
b. Design matrix
c. Hankel matrix
d. Diagonal Matrix

Chapter 2. LINEAR SYSTEMS

26. In mathematics, the _____ of a number n is the number that, when added to n, yields zero. The _____ of n is denoted −n. For example, 7 is −7, because 7 + (−7) = 0, and the _____ of −0.3 is 0.3, because −0.3 + 0.3 = 0.
    a. Arity
    b. Algebraic structure
    c. Additive inverse
    d. Associativity

27. _____s is the social science that studies the production, distribution, and consumption of goods and services.

    The term _____s comes from the Ancient Greek oá¼°κονομῐα (oikonomia, 'management of a household, administration') from oá¼¶κος (oikos, 'house') + vĭŒμος (nomos, 'custom' or 'law'), hence 'rules of the house(hold)'.

    Current _____ models developed out of the broader field of political economy in the late 19th century, owing to a desire to use an empirical approach more akin to the physical sciences.

    a. A chemical equation
    b. A Mathematical Theory of Communication
    c. Economic
    d. Experimental economics

28. In statistics, _____ is a form of regression analysis in which the relationship between one or more independent variables and another variable, called dependent variable, is modeled by a least squares function, called _____ equation. This function is a linear combination of one or more model parameters, called regression coefficients. A _____ equation with one independent variable represents a straight line.
    a. Random variables
    b. Kurtosis
    c. Percentile rank
    d. Linear regression

29. A _____ is a type of display using Cartesian coordinates to display values for two variables for a set of data. The data is displayed as a collection of points, each having the value of one variable determining the position on the horizontal axis and the value of the other variable determining the position on the vertical axis. A _____ is also called a scatter chart, scatter diagram and scatter graph.
    a. 120-cell
    b. 1-center problem
    c. 2-3 heap
    d. Scatter plot

Chapter 2. LINEAR SYSTEMS

30. A _____ is is a graphical technique for presenting a data set drawn by hand or produced by a mechanical or electronic plotter. It is a graph depicting the relationship between two or more variables used, for instance, in visualising scientific data.

_____s play an important role in statistics and data analysis.

a. Lattice
b. Dini
c. C-35
d. Plot

31. The _____ fallacy is an informal fallacy. It ascribes cause where none exists. The flaw is failing to account for natural fluctuations.
a. Depth
b. Degrees of freedom
c. Differential
d. Regression

32. The method of _____ or ordinary _____ is used to solve overdetermined systems. _____ is often applied in statistical contexts, particularly regression analysis.

_____ can be interpreted as a method of fitting data.

a. Non-linear least squares
b. System equivalence
c. Rata Die
d. Least squares

33. The mathematical concept of a _____ expresses the intuitive idea of deterministic dependence between two quantities, one of which is viewed as primary and the other as secondary. A _____ then is a way to associate a unique output for each input of a specified type, for example, a real number or an element of a given set.
a. Grill
b. Coherent
c. Going up
d. Function

Chapter 3. LINEAR PROGRAMMING

1. In mathematics and computer science, an optimization problem is the problem of finding the best solution from all feasible solutions. More formally, an optimization problem A is a quadruple , where

   - I is a set of instances;
   - given an instance ☒ >, f is the set of feasible solutions;
   - given an instance x and a feasible solution y of x, m denotes the measure of y, which is usually a positive real.
   - g is the goal function, and is either min or max.

   The goal is then to find for some instance x an _____, that is, a feasible solution y with

   ☒ >

   For each optimization problem, there is a corresponding decision problem that asks whether there is a feasible solution for some particular measure m_0. For example, if there is a graph G which contains vertices u and v, an optimization problem might be 'find a path from u to v that uses the fewest edges'. This problem might have an answer of, say, 4.

   a. Interactive proof system
   b. Exponential time
   c. Approximation algorithms
   d. Optimal solution

2. In mathematics, an _____ is a statement about the relative size or order of two objects, or about whether they are the same or not

   - The notation a < b means that a is less than b.
   - The notation a > b means that a is greater than b.
   - The notation a ≠ b means that a is not equal to b, but does not say that one is bigger than the other or even that they can be compared in size.

   In all these cases, a is not equal to b, hence, '_____'.

   These relations are known as strict _____

   - The notation a ≤ b means that a is less than or equal to b;
   - The notation a ≥ b means that a is greater than or equal to b;

An additional use of the notation is to show that one quantity is much greater than another, normally by several orders of magnitude.

- The notation a << b means that a is much less than b.
- The notation a >> b means that a is much greater than b.

If the sense of the _____ is the same for all values of the variables for which its members are defined, then the _____ is called an 'absolute' or 'unconditional' _____. If the sense of an _____ holds only for certain values of the variables involved, but is reversed or destroyed for other values of the variables, it is called a conditional _____.

An _____ may appear unsolvable because it only states whether a number is larger or smaller than another number; but it is possible to apply the same operations for equalities to inequalities. For example, to find x for the _____ 10x > 23 one would divide 23 by 10.

a. Inequality
b. A posteriori
c. A Mathematical Theory of Communication
d. A chemical equation

3. In mathematics a _____ is an inequality which involves a linear function.

When operating in terms of real numbers, linear inequalities are the ones written in the forms

$$f(x) < b \text{ or } f(x) \leq b,$$

where f(x) is a linear functional in real numbers and b is a constant real number. Alternatively, these may be viewed as

$$g(x) < 0 \text{ or } g(x) \leq 0,$$

where g(x) is an affine function.

a. Generalized singular value decomposition
b. Split-complex number
c. Linear inequality
d. Levi-Civita symbol

Chapter 3. LINEAR PROGRAMMING

4. In mathematics, _____ is a technique for optimization of a linear objective function, subject to linear equality and linear inequality constraints. Informally, _____ determines the way to achieve the best outcome in a given mathematical model given some list of requirements represented as linear equations.

More formally, given a polytope, and a real-valued affine function

$$f(x_1, x_2, \ldots, x_n) = c_1 x_1 + c_2 x_2 + \cdots + c_n x_n + d$$

defined on this polytope, a _____ method will find a point in the polytope where this function has the smallest value.

a. Linear programming relaxation
b. Descent direction
c. Linear programming
d. Lin-Kernighan

5. _____ is either of the two parts into which a plane divides the three-dimensional space. More generally, a _____ is either of the two parts into which a hyperplane divides an affine space.

a. Pendent
b. Half-space
c. Parallelogram law
d. Simple polytope

6. In mathematics, a _____ is, informally, an infinitely vast and infinitely thin sheet. _____s may be thought of as objects in some higher dimensional space, or they may be considered without any outside space, as in the setting of Euclidean geometry

a. Group
b. Blocking
c. Bandwidth
d. Plane

7. In optimization, a candidate solution is a member of a set of possible solutions to a given problem. A candidate solution does not have to be a likely or reasonable solution to the problem. The space of all candidate solutions is called the _____, feasible set, search space, or solution space.

Chapter 3. LINEAR PROGRAMMING

a. Step response
b. Leapfrog integration
c. Quadratic eigenvalue problem
d. Feasible region

8. In topology, the _____ of a subset S of a topological space X is the set of points which can be approached both from S and from the outside of S. More formally, it is the set of points in the closure of S, not belonging to the interior of S. An element of the _____ of S is called a _____ point of S.
   a. Boundary
   b. Heap
   c. Character
   d. Bertrand paradox

9. A set S of real numbers is called _____ from above if there is a real number k such that $k \geq s$ for all s in S. The number k is called an upper bound of S. The terms _____ from below and lower bound are similarly defined.
   a. Bounded
   b. Descent
   c. Derivative algebra
   d. Harmonic series

10. In mathematics, a _____ is a condition that a solution to an optimization problem must satisfy. There are two types of _____s: equality _____s and inequality _____s. The set of solutions that satisfy all _____s is called the feasible set.
    a. Concurrent
    b. Foci
    c. Decidable
    d. Constraint

11. An _____ is a tree data structure in which each internal node has up to eight children. _____s are most often used to partition a three dimensional space by recursively subdividing it into eight octants. _____s are the three-dimensional analog of quadtrees.
    a. External node
    b. Adaptive k-d tree
    c. Interval tree
    d. Octree

12. The mathematical concept of a _____ expresses the intuitive idea of deterministic dependence between two quantities, one of which is viewed as primary and the other as secondary. A _____ then is a way to associate a unique output for each input of a specified type, for example, a real number or an element of a given set.

   a. Coherent
   b. Grill
   c. Going up
   d. Function

13. In geometry, a _____ or n-_____ is an n-dimensional analogue of a triangle. Specifically, a _____ is the convex hull of a set of affinely independent points in some Euclidean space of dimension n or higher.

For example, a 0-_____ is a point, a 1-_____ is a line segment, a 2-_____ is a triangle, a 3-_____ is a tetrahedron, and a 4-_____ is a pentachoron.

   a. Simplex
   b. Hypercell
   c. Demihypercubes
   d. Polytetrahedron

14. In mathematical optimization theory, the simplex algorithm, created by the American mathematician George Dantzig in 1947, is a popular algorithm for numerical solution of the linear programming problem. The journal Computing in Science and Engineering listed it as one of the top 10 algorithms of the century.

An unrelated, but similarly named method is the Nelder-Mead method or downhill _____ due to Nelder ' Mead and is a numerical method for optimising many-dimensional unconstrained problems, belonging to the more general class of search algorithms.

   a. Differential evolution
   b. Fibonacci search
   c. Hill climbing
   d. Simplex method

15. _____ and independent variables refer to values that change in relationship to each other. The _____ are those that are observed to change in response to the independent variables. The independent variables are those that are deliberately manipulated to invoke a change in the _____.

a. Round robin test
b. Steiner system
c. Yates analysis
d. Dependent variables

16. Dependent variables and _____ refer to values that change in relationship to each other. The dependent variables are those that are observed to change in response to the _____. The _____ are those that are deliberately manipulated to invoke a change in the dependent variables.
   a. Operational confound
   b. One-factor-at-a-time method
   c. Independent variables
   d. Experimental design diagram

Chapter 4. LINEAR PROGRAMMING: THE SIMPLEX METHOD

1. In geometry, a _____ or n-_____ is an n-dimensional analogue of a triangle. Specifically, a _____ is the convex hull of a set of affinely independent points in some Euclidean space of dimension n or higher.

For example, a 0-_____ is a point, a 1-_____ is a line segment, a 2-_____ is a triangle, a 3-_____ is a tetrahedron, and a 4-_____ is a pentachoron.

   a. Polytetrahedron
   b. Simplex
   c. Hypercell
   d. Demihypercubes

2. In mathematical optimization theory, the simplex algorithm, created by the American mathematician George Dantzig in 1947, is a popular algorithm for numerical solution of the linear programming problem. The journal Computing in Science and Engineering listed it as one of the top 10 algorithms of the century.

An unrelated, but similarly named method is the Nelder-Mead method or downhill _____ due to Nelder ' Mead and is a numerical method for optimising many-dimensional unconstrained problems, belonging to the more general class of search algorithms.

   a. Simplex method
   b. Hill climbing
   c. Fibonacci search
   d. Differential evolution

3. In mathematics, _____ is a technique for optimization of a linear objective function, subject to linear equality and linear inequality constraints. Informally, _____ determines the way to achieve the best outcome in a given mathematical model given some list of requirements represented as linear equations.

More formally, given a polytope, and a real-valued affine function

$$f(x_1, x_2, \ldots, x_n) = c_1 x_1 + c_2 x_2 + \cdots + c_n x_n + d$$

defined on this polytope, a _____ method will find a point in the polytope where this function has the smallest value.

   a. Lin-Kernighan
   b. Linear programming relaxation
   c. Descent direction
   d. Linear programming

Chapter 4. LINEAR PROGRAMMING: THE SIMPLEX METHOD

4. In Linear programming a _____ is a variable which is added to a constraint to turn the inequality into an equation. This is required to turn an inequality into an equality where a linear combination of variables is less than or equal to a given constant in the former. As with the other variables in the augmented constraints, the _____ cannot take on negative values, as the Simplex algorithm requires them to be positive or zero.
   a. Shekel function
   b. Bellman equation
   c. Slack variable
   d. Shape optimization

5. In optimization, a candidate solution is a member of a set of possible solutions to a given problem. A candidate solution does not have to be a likely or reasonable solution to the problem. The space of all candidate solutions is called the _____, feasible set, search space, or solution space.
   a. Quadratic eigenvalue problem
   b. Feasible region
   c. Step response
   d. Leapfrog integration

6. In mathematical optimization theory, the _____, created by the North American mathematician George Dantzig in 1947, is a popular technique for numerical solution of the linear programming problem.
   a. Feit–Thompson theorem
   b. Simplex algorithm
   c. Partition
   d. Sociable number

7. Initial objects are also called _____, and terminal objects are also called final.
   a. Direct limit
   b. Terminal object
   c. Colimit
   d. Coterminal

8. In mathematics, an _____ or member of a set is any one of the distinct objects that make up that set.

Writing A = {1,2,3,4}, means that the _____s of the set A are the numbers 1, 2, 3 and 4. Groups of _____s of A, for example {1,2}, are subsets of A.

a. Ideal
b. Universal code
c. Element
d. Order

9. In the mathematical area of order theory, every partially ordered set P gives rise to a _____ partially ordered set which is often denoted by P^{op} or P^d. This _____ order P^{op} is defined to be the set with the inverse order. It is easy to see that this construction, which can be depicted by flipping the Hasse diagram for P upside down, will indeed yield a partially ordered set.
   a. Christofides heuristics
   b. Dual
   c. Contraction mapping
   d. Context-sensitive language

10. In linear programming, the primary problem and the _____ are complementary. A solution to either one determines a solution to both.

Linear programming problems are optimization problems in which the objective function and the constraints are all linear.

   a. Topological derivative
   b. Linear matrix inequality
   c. Linear programming relaxation
   d. Dual problem

11. In mathematics, a _____ is a rectangular table of elements, which may be numbers or, more generally, any abstract quantities that can be added and multiplied. Matrices are used to describe linear equations, keep track of the coefficients of linear transformations and to record data that depend on multiple parameters. Matrices are described by the field of _____ theory.
   a. Coherent
   b. Double counting
   c. Matrix
   d. Compression

Chapter 4. LINEAR PROGRAMMING: THE SIMPLEX METHOD

12. In linear algebra, the _____ of a matrix A is another matrix A^T created by any one of the following equivalent actions:

    - write the rows of A as the columns of A^T
    - write the columns of A as the rows of A^T
    - reflect A by its main diagonal to obtain A^T

Formally, the _____ of an m × n matrix A is the n × m matrix

$$\mathbf{A}^T_{ij} = \mathbf{A}_{ji} \text{ for } 1 \leq i \leq n, 1 \leq j \leq m.$$

- $\begin{bmatrix} 1 & 2 \\ 3 & 4 \end{bmatrix}^T = \begin{bmatrix} 1 & 3 \\ 2 & 4 \end{bmatrix}.$

- $\begin{bmatrix} 1 & 2 \\ 3 & 4 \\ 5 & 6 \end{bmatrix}^T = \begin{bmatrix} 1 & 3 & 5 \\ 2 & 4 & 6 \end{bmatrix}.$

For matrices A, B and scalar c we have the following properties of _____:

1. $\left(\mathbf{A}^T\right)^T = \mathbf{A}$

    Taking the _____ is an involution.

- $(\mathbf{A} + \mathbf{B})^T = \mathbf{A}^T + \mathbf{B}^T$

    The _____ respects addition.

- $(\mathbf{AB})^T = \mathbf{B}^T \mathbf{A}^T$

    Note that the order of the factors reverses. From this one can deduce that a square matrix A is invertible if and only if A^T is invertible, and in this case we have^T =$^{-1}$. It is relatively easy to extend this result to the general case of multiple matrices, where we find that^T = $Z^T Y^T X^T ... C^T B^T A^T$.

- $(c\mathbf{A})^T = c\mathbf{A}^T$

Chapter 4. LINEAR PROGRAMMING: THE SIMPLEX METHOD

The _____ of a scalar is the same scalar. Together with, this states that the _____ is a linear map from the space of m × n matrices to the space of all n × m matrices.

- $\det(\mathbf{A}^T) = \det(\mathbf{A})$

  The determinant of a matrix is the same as that of its _____.

- The dot product of two column vectors a and b can be computed as

  $$\mathbf{a} \cdot \mathbf{b} = \mathbf{a}^T \mathbf{b},$$

which is written as $a_i\, b^i$ in Einstein notation.
- If A has only real entries, then $A^T A$ is a positive-semidefinite matrix.
- $(\mathbf{A}^T)^{-1} = (\mathbf{A}^{-1})^T$

  The _____ of an invertible matrix is also invertible, and its inverse is the _____ of the inverse of the original matrix.

- If A is a square matrix, then its eigenvalues are equal to the eigenvalues of its _____.

A square matrix whose _____ is equal to itself is called a symmetric matrix; that is, A is symmetric if

$$\mathbf{A}^T = \mathbf{A}.$$

A square matrix whose _____ is also its inverse is called an orthogonal matrix; that is, G is orthogonal if

$$\mathbf{G}\mathbf{G}^T = \mathbf{G}^T\mathbf{G} = \mathbf{I}_n,$$ the identity matrix.

A square matrix whose _____ is equal to its negative is called skew-symmetric matrix; that is, A is skew-symmetric if

$$\mathbf{A}^T = -\mathbf{A}.$$

The conjugate _____ of the complex matrix A, written as A^*, is obtained by taking the _____ of A and the complex conjugate of each entry:

$$\mathbf{A}^* = (\overline{\mathbf{A}})^T = \overline{(\mathbf{A}^T)}.$$

Chapter 4. LINEAR PROGRAMMING: THE SIMPLEX METHOD

If f: V→W is a linear map between vector spaces V and W with nondegenerate bilinear forms, we define the _____ of f to be the linear map $^t f$: W→V, determined by

$$B_V(v, {}^t f(w)) = B_W(f(v), w) \quad \forall\ v \in V, w \in W.$$

Here, B_V and B_W are the bilinear forms on V and W respectively. The matrix of the _____ of a map is the transposed matrix only if the bases are orthonormal with respect to their bilinear forms.

Over a complex vector space, one often works with sesquilinear forms instead of bilinear.

a. Polynomial matrix
b. Tridiagonal matrix
c. Cartan matrix
d. Transpose

13. In the geometry of the projective plane, _____ refers to geometric transformations that replace points by lines and lines by points while preserving incidence properties among the transformed objects. The existence of such transformations leads to a general principle, that any theorem about incidences between points and lines in the projective plane may be transformed into another theorem about lines and points, by a substitution of the appropriate words.

_____ in the projective plane is a special case of _____ for projective spaces, transformations that interchange

dimension + codimension.

a. Duality
b. Disk
c. Blocking
d. Decidable

14. In mathematics, a _____ is a statement that can be proved on the basis of explicitly stated or previously agreed assumptions.
a. Logical value
b. Boolean function
c. Disjunction introduction
d. Theorem

15. In mathematics, a _____ is a condition that a solution to an optimization problem must satisfy. There are two types of _____s: equality _____s and inequality _____s. The set of solutions that satisfy all _____s is called the feasible set.

a. Decidable
b. Foci
c. Concurrent
d. Constraint

16. _____ is the study of how the variation in the output of a mathematical model can be apportioned, qualitatively or quantitatively, to different sources of variation in the input of a model.

In more general terms uncertainty and sensitivity analyses investigate the robustness of a study when the study includes some form of mathematical modelling. While uncertainty analysis studies the overall uncertainty in the conclusions of the study, _____ tries to identify what source of uncertainty weights more on the study's conclusions.

a. 1-center problem
b. Sensitivity analysis
c. 2-3 heap
d. 120-cell

Chapter 5. MATHEMATICS Of FINANCE

1. _____ is a fee, paid on borrowed capital. Assets lent include money, shares, consumer goods through hire purchase, major assets such as aircraft, and even entire factories in finance lease arrangements. The _____ is calculated upon the value of the assets in the same manner as upon money.
   a. Interest
   b. Interest sensitivity gap
   c. A Mathematical Theory of Communication
   d. Interest expense

2. In abstract algebra, a module S over a ring R is called _____ or irreducible if it is not the zero module 0 and if its only submodules are 0 and S. Understanding the _____ modules over a ring is usually helpful because these modules form the 'building blocks' of all other modules in a certain sense.

   Abelian groups are the same as Z-modules.

   a. Basis
   b. Harmonic series
   c. Derivation
   d. Simple

3. _____ is the concept of adding accumulated interest back to the principal, so that interest is earned on interest from that moment on. The act of declaring interest to be principal is called compounding. A loan, for example, may have its interest compounded every month: in this case, a loan with $100 principal and 1% interest per month would have a balance of $101 at the end of the first month.
   a. Net interest margin
   b. Retained interest
   c. Net interest margin securities
   d. Compound interest

4. In mathematics, a _____ is a number that can be expressed as an integral of an algebraic function over an algebraic domain. Kontsevich and Zagier define a _____ as a complex number whose real and imaginary parts are values of absolutely convergent integrals of rational functions with rational coefficients, over domains in given by polynomial inequalities with rational coefficients.
   a. Period
   b. Boussinesq approximation
   c. Disk
   d. Closeness

Chapter 5. MATHEMATICS Of FINANCE

5. _____ or amortisation is the process of decreasing an amount over a period of time. The word comes from Middle English amortisen to kill, alienate in mortmain, from Anglo-French amorteser, alteration of amortir, from Vulgar Latin admortire to kill, from Latin ad- + mort-, mors death. Particular instances of the term include:

- _____, the allocation of a lump sum amount to different time periods, particularly for loans and other forms of finance, including related interest or other finance charges.
    - _____ schedule, a table detailing each periodic payment on a loan, as generated by an _____ calculator.
    - Negative _____, an _____ schedule where the loan amount actually increases through not paying the full interest
- Amortized analysis, analyzing the execution cost of algorithms over a sequence of operations.
- _____ of capital expenditures of certain assets under accounting rules, particularly intangible assets, in a manner analogous to depreciation.
- _____

_____ is also used in the context of zoning regulations and describes the time in which a property owner has to relocate when the property's use constitutes a preexisting nonconforming use under zoning regulations.

- Depreciation

a. ISAAC
b. Identity
c. Origin
d. Amortization

6. _____ is that which is owed; usually referencing assets owed, but the term can cover other obligations. In the case of assets, _____ is a means of using future purchasing power in the present before a summation has been earned.
a. Debt
b. Cobb-Douglas
c. Metaheuristic
d. Point-slope form

7. An _____ is a table detailing each periodic payment on a amortizing loan, as generated by an amortization calculator.

While a portion of every payment is applied towards both the interest and the principal balance of the loan, the exact amount applied to principal each time varies. An _____ reveals the specific monetary amount put towards interest, as well as the specific put towards the Principal balance, with each payment.

a. A chemical equation
b. Accounts receivable
c. A Mathematical Theory of Communication
d. Amortization schedule

8. A _____ is the transfer of an interest in property (or in law the equivalent - a charge) to a lender as a security for a debt - usually a loan of money. While a _____ in itself is not a debt, it is lender's security for a debt. It is a transfer of an interest in land (or the equivalent), from the owner to the _____ lender, on the condition that this interest will be returned to the owner of the real estate when the terms of the _____ have been satisfied or performed.

a. Mortgage
b. 1-center problem
c. 2-3 heap
d. 120-cell

9. _____ is the concept or idea of fairness in economics, particularly as to taxation or welfare economics.

a. Event
b. Union
c. Interval
d. Equity

10. The terms _____, nominal APR, and effective APR describe the interest rate for a whole year, rather than just a monthly fee/rate, as applied on a loan, mortgage, credit card, etc. Those terms have formal, legal definitions in some countries or legal jurisdictions, but in general:

- The nominal APR is the simple-interest rate.
- The effective APR is the fee+compound interest rate.

The nominal APR is calculated as: the rate, for a payment period, multiplied by the number of payment periods in a year. However, the exact legal definition of 'effective APR' can vary greatly in each jurisdiction, depending on the type of fees included, such as participation fees, loan origination fees, monthly service charges, or late fees. The effective APR has been called the 'mathematically-true' interest rate for each year. The computation for the effective APR, as the fee+compound interest rate, can also vary depending on whether the up-front fees, such as origination or participation fees, are added to the entire amount, or treated as a short-term loan due in the first payment.

a. A posteriori
b. A Mathematical Theory of Communication
c. Annual percentage rate
d. A chemical equation

11. In mathematics, a _____ is a way of expressing a number as a fraction of 100. It is often denoted using the percent sign, '%'. For example, 45% is equal to 45 / 100, or 0.45.
a. Lowest common denominator
b. Least common multiple
c. Subtrahend
d. Percentage

Chapter 6. SETS AND COUNTING

1. In mathematics, an _____ or member of a set is any one of the distinct objects that make up that set.

Writing A = {1,2,3,4}, means that the _____s of the set A are the numbers 1, 2, 3 and 4. Groups of _____s of A, for example {1,2}, are subsets of A.

   a. Order
   b. Universal code
   c. Element
   d. Ideal

2. In mathematics, a _____ is a rectangular table of elements, which may be numbers or, more generally, any abstract quantities that can be added and multiplied. Matrices are used to describe linear equations, keep track of the coefficients of linear transformations and to record data that depend on multiple parameters. Matrices are described by the field of _____ theory.
   a. Double counting
   b. Compression
   c. Coherent
   d. Matrix

3. In mathematics, and more specifically set theory, the _____ is the unique set having no members. Some axiomatic set theories assure that the _____ exists by including an axiom of _____; in other theories, its existence can be deduced. Many possible properties of sets are trivially true for the _____.
   a. Inverse function
   b. Empty set
   c. Empty function
   d. A Mathematical Theory of Communication

4. In mathematics, especially in set theory, a set A is a _____ of a set B if A is 'contained' inside B. Notice that A and B may coincide. The relationship of one set being a _____ of another is called inclusion.
   a. Cartesian product
   b. Horizontal line test
   c. Subset
   d. Set of all sets

5. In mathematics, and particularly in applications to set theory and the foundations of mathematics, a _____ or universal class is a class that contains all of the elements and sets that one may wish to use in a given situation. There are several versions of this general idea, described in the following sections.

Chapter 6. SETS AND COUNTING

Perhaps the simplest version is that any set can be a _____, so long as the object of study is confined to that particular set.

   a. Operation
   b. A Mathematical Theory of Communication
   c. A chemical equation
   d. Universe

6. _____ or set diagrams are diagrams that show all hypothetically possible logical relations between a finite collection of sets. _____ were invented around 1880 by John Venn. They are used in many fields, including set theory, probability, logic, statistics, and computer science.
   a. Venn diagrams
   b. 2-3 heap
   c. 1-center problem
   d. 120-cell

7. A _____ is a 2D geometric symbolic representation of information according to some visualization technique. Sometimes, the technique uses a 3D visualization which is then projected onto the 2D surface. The word graph is sometimes used as a synonym for _____.
   a. 120-cell
   b. Diagram
   c. 2-3 heap
   d. 1-center problem

8. An _____ is one that cannot be compressed because it lacks sufficient repeating sequences. Whether a string is compressible will often depend on the algorithm being used. Some examples may illuminate this.
   a. Incompressible string
   b. Entropy encoding
   c. A Mathematical Theory of Communication
   d. Arithmetic coding

9. In set theory, the term _____ refers to a set operation used in the convergence of set elements to form a resultant set containing the elements of both sets. As a simple example, a _____ of two disjoint sets, which do not have elements in common results in a set containing all elements from both sets. A Venn diagram representing the _____ of sets A and B.

a. UES
b. Introduction
c. Event
d. Union

10. In mathematics, the _____ of two sets A and B is the set that contains all elements of A that also belong to B, but no other elements.

For explanation of the symbols used in this article, refer to the table of mathematical symbols.

The _____ of A and B

The _____ of A and B is written 'A ∩ B'. Formally:

>   x is an element of A ∩ B if and only if
>   - x is an element of A and
>   - x is an element of B.
>
>   For example:
>   - The _____ of the sets {1, 2, 3} and {2, 3, 4} is {2, 3}.
>   - The number 9 is not in the _____ of the set of prime numbers {2, 3, 5, 7, 11, …} and the set of odd numbers {1, 3, 5, 7, 9, 11, …}.

If the _____ of two sets A and B is empty, that is they have no elements in common, then they are said to be disjoint, denoted: A ∩ B = ∅. For example the sets {1, 2} and {3, 4} are disjoint, written
{1, 2} ∩ {3, 4} = ∅.

a. Order
b. Erlang
c. Intersection
d. Advice

11. In discrete mathematics and predominantly in set theory, a _____ is a concept used in comparisons of sets to refer to the unique values of one set in relation to another. The terms 'absolute' and 'relative' _____ refer to more specific applications of the concept, with universal _____s referring to elements unique to the universal set and the latter referring to the unique elements of one set in relation to another. In this image, the universal set is represented by the border of the image, and the set A as a disc.

a. Complement
b. Kernel
c. Huge
d. Derivative algebra

12. In mathematics, two sets are said to be disjoint if they have no element in common. For example, {1, 2, 3} and {4, 5, 6} are _____.

Formally, two sets A and B are disjoint if their intersection is the empty set.
wikimedia.org/math/b/3/5/b35d3befc06b831ff4d6cd63bf922efb.png">

This definition extends to any collection of sets.

a. Horizontal line test
b. Disjoint sets
c. Subset
d. Preimage

13. In set theory, a _____ is a partially ordered set such that for each $t \in T$, the set $\{s \in T : s < t\}$ is well-ordered by the relation <. For each $t \in T$, the order type of $\{s \in T : s < t\}$ is called the height of t. The height of T itself is the least ordinal greater than the height of each element of T.

a. Set-theoretic topology
b. Tree
c. Definable numbers
d. Transitive reduction

14. _____ is the mathematical operation of scaling one number by another. It is one of the four basic operations in elementary arithmetic.

_____ is defined for whole numbers in terms of repeated addition; for example, 4 multiplied by 3 can be calculated by adding 3 copies of 4 together:

$$4 + 4 + 4 = 12.$$

_____ of rational numbers and real numbers is defined by systematic generalization of this basic idea.

a. The number 0 is even.
b. Multiplication
c. Highest common factor
d. Least common multiple

15. A _____ is a structure built to span a gorge, valley, road, railroad track, river, body of water for the purpose of providing passage over the obstacle. Designs of _____s will vary depending on the function of the _____ and the nature of the terrain where the _____ is to be constructed. Roman _____ of Córdoba, Spain, built in the 1st century BC. Ponte di Pietra in Verona, Italy. A log _____ in the French Alps near Vallorcine. An English 18th century example of a _____ in the Palladian style, with shops on the span: Pulteney _____, Bath A Han Dynasty Chinese miniature model of two residential towers joined by a _____

The first _____s were made by nature -- as simple as a log fallen across a stream.

a. 1-center problem
b. Bridge
c. 2-3 heap
d. 120-cell

16. In several fields of mathematics the term _____ is used with different but closely related meanings. They all relate to the notion of mapping the elements of a set to other elements of the same set, i.e., exchanging elements of a set.

The general concept of _____ can be defined more formally in different contexts:

In combinatorics, a _____ is usually understood to be a sequence containing each element from a finite set once, and only once.

a. Tensor product
b. Cyclic permutation
c. Linearly independent
d. Permutation

17. In mathematics, the _____ of a non-negative integer n, denoted by n!, is the product of all positive integers less than or equal to n. For example,

$$5! = 1 \times 2 \times 3 \times 4 \times 5 = 120$$

and

$$6! = 1 \times 2 \times 3 \times 4 \times 5 \times 6 = 720$$

The notation n! was introduced by Christian Kramp in 1808.

The _____ function is formally defined by

$$n! = \prod_{k=1}^{n} k \qquad \forall n \in \mathbb{N}.$$

The above definition incorporates the instance

$$0! = 1$$

as an instance of the fact that the product of no numbers at all is 1.

a. Symbolic combinatorics
b. Plane partition
c. Partition of a set
d. Factorial

18. In simple terms, two events are _____ if they cannot occur at the same time.

In logic, two _____ propositions are propositions that logically cannot both be true. To say that more than two propositions are _____ may, depending on context mean that no two of them can both be true, or only that they cannot all be true.

a. Philosophy of mathematics
b. Determinism
c. Philosophy
d. Mutually exclusive

19. _____ is the likelihood or chance that something is the case or will happen. Theoretical _____ is used extensively in areas such as statistics, mathematics, science and philosophy to draw conclusions about the likelihood of potential events and the underlying mechanics of complex systems.

Chapter 6. SETS AND COUNTING

The word _____ does not have a consistent direct definition.

- a. Probability
- b. Discrete random variable
- c. Statistical significance
- d. Standardized moment

20. In category theory, an abstract branch of mathematics, an _____ of a category C is an object I in C such that for every object X in C, there exists precisely one morphism I → X. The dual notion is that of a terminal object: T is terminal if for every object X in C there exists a single morphism X → T. _____s are also called coterminal, and terminal objects are also called final.
    - a. Initial object
    - b. A chemical equation
    - c. A Mathematical Theory of Communication
    - d. A posteriori

21. In combinatorial mathematics, a _____ is an un-ordered collection of distinct elements, usually of a prescribed size and taken from a given set. Given such a set S, a _____ of elements of S is just a subset of S, where as always forsets the order of the elements is not taken into account. Also, as always forsets, no elements can be repeated more than once in a _____; this is often referred to as a 'collection without repetition'.
    - a. Fill-in
    - b. Sparsity
    - c. Heawood number
    - d. Combination

22. In elementary algebra, a _____ is a polynomial with two terms: the sum of two monomials. It is the simplest kind of polynomial except for a monomial.

The _____ $a^2 - b^2$ can be factored as the product of two other _____s:

$a^2 - b^2$.

The product of a pair of linear _____s a x + b and c x + d is:

2 +x + bd.

Chapter 6. SETS AND COUNTING

A _____ raised to the nth power, represented as

n

can be expanded by means of the _____ theorem or, equivalently, using Pascal's triangle.

a. Cylindrical algebraic decomposition
b. Real structure
c. Rational root theorem
d. Binomial

23. In mathematics, the _____ is an important formula giving the expansion of powers of sums. Its simplest version states that

$$(x+y)^n = \sum_{k=0}^{n} \binom{n}{k} x^{n-k} y^k \qquad (1)$$

for any real or complex numbers x and y, and any nonnegative integer n. The binomial coefficient appearing in may be defined in terms of the factorial function n!:

$$\binom{n}{k} = \frac{n!}{k!(n-k)!}.$$

For example, here are the cases where 2 ≤ n ≤ 5:

$$(x+y)^2 = x^2 + 2xy + y^2$$
$$(x+y)^3 = x^3 + 3x^2y + 3xy^2 + y^3$$
$$(x+y)^4 = x^4 + 4x^3y + 6x^2y^2 + 4xy^3 + y^4$$
$$(x+y)^5 = x^5 + 5x^4y + 10x^3y^2 + 10x^2y^3 + 5xy^4 + y^5.$$

Formula is valid more generally for any elements x and y of a semiring as long as xy = yx..

a. Hypergeometric identities
b. Stirling transform
c. Lah numbers
d. Binomial theorem

Chapter 6. SETS AND COUNTING

24. In mathematics, a _____ is a statement that can be proved on the basis of explicitly stated or previously agreed assumptions.
    a. Disjunction introduction
    b. Boolean function
    c. Logical value
    d. Theorem

25. In _____, the probability of many events can be determined by direct calculation In most cases, the probabilities and odds are approximations due to rounding.
    a. 2-3 heap
    b. 120-cell
    c. 1-center problem
    d. Poker

26. In number theory, a _____ of a positive integer n is a way of writing n as a sum of positive integers. Two sums which only differ in the order of their summands are considered to be the same _____; if order matters then the sum becomes a composition. A summand in a _____ is also called a part.
    a. Derivative algebra
    b. Congruent
    c. Distribution
    d. Partition

27. In quantum field theory and statistical mechanics in the thermodynamic limit, a system with a global symmetry can have more than one phase. For parameters where the symmetry is spontaneously broken, the system is said to be _____. When the global symmetry is unbroken the system is disordered.
    a. Ursell function
    b. Einstein relation
    c. Isoenthalpic-isobaric ensemble
    d. Ordered

28. In combinatorial mathematics, an _____ O of a set S is a sequence

    $A_1, A_2, A_3, ..., A_n$

of subsets of S, with union is S, which are non-empty, and pairwise disjoint. This differs from a partition of a set, in that the order of the A_i matters.

For example, one _____ of { 1, 2, 3, 4, 5 } is

{1, 2} {3, 4} {5}

which is equivalent to

{1, 2} {4, 3} {5}

but distinct from

{3, 4} {1, 2} {5}.

a. Eulerian number
b. Ordered Partition
c. Association scheme
d. Enumeration

Chapter 7. PROBABILITY

1. _____ IPA: [pjɛʁ ɛ dɘ™fɛʁ 'ma] (17 August 1601 or 1607/8 - 12 January 1665) was a French lawyer at the Parlement of Toulouse, France, and a mathematician who is given credit for early developments that led to modern calculus. In particular, he is recognized for his discovery of an original method of finding the greatest and the smallest ordinates of curved lines, which is analogous to that of the then unknown differential calculus, as well as his research into the theory of numbers. He also made notable contributions to analytic geometry, probability, and optics.
   a. Felix Hausdorff
   b. Philip J. Davis
   c. Nikita Borisov
   d. Pierre de Fermat

2. _____ is the likelihood or chance that something is the case or will happen. Theoretical _____ is used extensively in areas such as statistics, mathematics, science and philosophy to draw conclusions about the likelihood of potential events and the underlying mechanics of complex systems.

   The word _____ does not have a consistent direct definition.

   a. Standardized moment
   b. Statistical significance
   c. Discrete random variable
   d. Probability

3. _____ is the branch of mathematics concerned with analysis of random phenomena. The central objects of _____ are random variables, stochastic processes, and events: mathematical abstractions of non-deterministic events or measured quantities that may either be single occurrences or evolve over time in an apparently random fashion. Although an individual coin toss or the roll of a die is a random event, if repeated many times the sequence of random events will exhibit certain statistical patterns, which can be studied and predicted.
   a. Probability theory
   b. Martingale central limit theorem
   c. Standard probability space
   d. Law of large numbers

4. The word _____ has many distinct meanings in different fields of knowledge, depending on their methodologies and the context of discussion. Broadly speaking we can say that a _____ is some kind of belief or claim that (supposedly) explains, asserts, or consolidates some class of claims. Additionally, in contrast with a theorem the statement of the _____ is generally accepted only in some tentative fashion as opposed to regarding it as having been conclusively established.

a. Defined
b. Transport of structure
c. Theory
d. Per mil

5. In scientific inquiry, an _____ is a method of investigating particular types of research questions or solving particular types of problems. The _____ is a cornerstone in the empirical approach to acquiring deeper knowledge about the world and is used in both natural sciences as well as in social sciences. An _____ is defined, in science, as a method of investigating less known fields, solving practical problems and proving theoretical assumptions.
   a. A posteriori
   b. A Mathematical Theory of Communication
   c. Experiment
   d. A chemical equation

6. In game theory, an _____ is a set of moves or strategies taken by the players, or their payoffs resulting from the actions or strategies taken by all players. The two are complementary in that given knowledge of the set of strategies of all players, the final state of the game is known, as are any relevant payoffs. In a game where chance or a random event is involved, the _____ is not known from only the set of strategies, but is only realized when the random even are realized.
   a. Algebraic
   b. Autonomous system
   c. Equaliser
   d. Outcome

7. The word _____ denotes information gained by means of observation, experience as opposed to theoretical. A central concept in science and the scientific method is that all evidence must be _____ that is, dependent on evidence or consequences that are observable by the senses. It is usually differentiated from the philosophic usage of empiricism by the use of the adjective '_____' or the adverb 'empirically.' '_____' as an adjective or adverb is used in conjunction with both the natural and social sciences, and refers to the use of working hypotheses that are testable using observation or experiment.
   a. Empirical
   b. A Mathematical Theory of Communication
   c. A posteriori
   d. A chemical equation

8. _____ or experimental probability, is the ratio of the number favorable outcomes to the total number of trials , not in a sample space but in an actual sequence of experiments. In a more general sense, _____ estimates probabilities from experience and observation. The phrase a posteriori probability has also been used an alternative to _____ or relative frequency.

a. Empirical probability
b. A chemical equation
c. A posteriori
d. A Mathematical Theory of Communication

9. In statistics the _____ of an event i is the number n_i of times the event occurred in the experiment or the study. These frequencies are often graphically represented in histograms.

We speak of absolute frequencies, when the counts n_i themselves are given and of

$$f_i = \frac{n_i}{N} = \frac{n_i}{\sum_i n_i}$$

Taking the f_i for all i and tabulating or plotting them leads to a _____ distribution.

a. Robinson-Dadson curves
b. Frequency
c. Digital room correction
d. Subharmonic

10. In mathematics and physics, there are a _____ number of topics named in honor of Leonhard Euler. As well, many of these topics include their own unique function, equation, formula, identity, number, or other mathematical entity. Unfortunately however, many of these entities have been given simple names like Euler's function, Euler's equation, and Euler's formula, which are further confused by variations of the 'Euler'-prefix Overall though, Euler's work touched upon so many fields that he is often the earliest written reference on a given matter.

a. List of mathematical knots and links
b. List of trigonometry topics
c. List of integrals of logarithmic functions
d. Large

11. The _____ is a theorem in probability that describes the long-term stability of the mean of a random variable. Given a random variable with a finite expected value, if its values are repeatedly sampled, as the number of these observations increases, their mean will tend to approach and stay close to the expected value.

The LLN can easily be illustrated using the rolls of a die.

Chapter 7. PROBABILITY

   a. Law of Large Numbers
   b. Point process
   c. Graphical model
   d. Random field

12. In statistics, a _____ is a subset of a population. Typically, the population is very large, making a census or a complete enumeration of all the values in the population impractical or impossible. The _____ represents a subset of manageable size.
   a. Duality
   b. Sample
   c. Boussinesq approximation
   d. Dispersion

13. In probability theory, the _____ or universal _____, often denoted S, Ω of an experiment or random trial is the set of all possible outcomes. For example, if the experiment is tossing a coin, the _____ is the set {head, tail}. For tossing a single six-sided die, the _____ is {1, 2, 3, 4, 5, 6}.
   a. Marginal distribution
   b. Martingale central limit theorem
   c. Sample space
   d. Markov chain

14. In abstract algebra, a module S over a ring R is called _____ or irreducible if it is not the zero module 0 and if its only submodules are 0 and S. Understanding the _____ modules over a ring is usually helpful because these modules form the 'building blocks' of all other modules in a certain sense.

Abelian groups are the same as Z-modules.

   a. Derivation
   b. Harmonic series
   c. Basis
   d. Simple

15. In probability theory, an _____ is a set of outcomes to which a probability is assigned. Typically, when the sample space is finite, any subset of the sample space is an _____. However, this approach does not work well in cases where the sample space is infinite, most notably when the outcome is a real number.

a. Information set
b. Audio compression
c. Equaliser
d. Event

16. _____ are small polyhedral objects, usually cubic, used for generating random numbers or other symbols. This makes _____ suitable as gambling devices, especially for craps or sic bo, or for use in non-gambling tabletop games.

A traditional die is a cube, marked on each of its six faces with a different number of circular patches or pits called pips.

a. 120-cell
b. 1-center problem
c. 2-3 heap
d. Dice

17. In discrete mathematics and predominantly in set theory, a _____ is a concept used in comparisons of sets to refer to the unique values of one set in relation to another. The terms 'absolute' and 'relative' _____ refer to more specific applications of the concept, with universal _____s referring to elements unique to the universal set and the latter referring to the unique elements of one set in relation to another. In this image, the universal set is represented by the border of the image, and the set A as a disc.
a. Derivative algebra
b. Kernel
c. Huge
d. Complement

18. In mathematics, the _____ of two sets A and B is the set that contains all elements of A that also belong to B, but no other elements.

For explanation of the symbols used in this article, refer to the table of mathematical symbols.

The _____ of A and B

The _____ of A and B is written 'A ∩ B'. Formally:

>x is an element of A ∩ B if and only if
>- x is an element of A and
>- x is an element of B.
>
>For example:
>- The _____ of the sets {1, 2, 3} and {2, 3, 4} is {2, 3}.
>- The number 9 is not in the _____ of the set of prime numbers {2, 3, 5, 7, 11, …} and the set of odd numbers {1, 3, 5, 7, 9, 11, …}.

If the _____ of two sets A and B is empty, that is they have no elements in common, then they are said to be disjoint, denoted: A ∩ B = ∅. For example the sets {1, 2} and {3, 4} are disjoint, written {1, 2} ∩ {3, 4} = ∅.

a. Erlang
b. Advice
c. Order
d. Intersection

19. In set theory, the term _____ refers to a set operation used in the convergence of set elements to form a resultant set containing the elements of both sets. As a simple example, a _____ of two disjoint sets, which do not have elements in common results in a set containing all elements from both sets. A Venn diagram representing the _____ of sets A and B.
a. UES
b. Introduction
c. Event
d. Union

20. In mathematics, a _____ is a statement that can be proved on the basis of explicitly stated or previously agreed assumptions.
a. Boolean function
b. Disjunction introduction
c. Logical value
d. Theorem

21. In simple terms, two events are _____ if they cannot occur at the same time.

Chapter 7. PROBABILITY

In logic, two _____ propositions are propositions that logically cannot both be true. To say that more than two propositions are _____ may, depending on context mean that no two of them can both be true, or only that they cannot all be true.

a. Philosophy of mathematics
b. Philosophy
c. Determinism
d. Mutually exclusive

22. In _____, the probability of many events can be determined by direct calculation In most cases, the probabilities and odds are approximations due to rounding.
a. 1-center problem
b. 120-cell
c. 2-3 heap
d. Poker

23. In combinatorial mathematics, a _____ is an un-ordered collection of distinct elements, usually of a prescribed size and taken from a given set. Given such a set S, a _____ of elements of S is just a subset of S, where as always forsets the order of the elements is not taken into account. Also, as always forsets, no elements can be repeated more than once in a _____; this is often referred to as a 'collection without repetition'.
a. Sparsity
b. Fill-in
c. Heawood number
d. Combination

24. _____ is the probability of some event A, given the occurrence of some other event B. _____ is written P[A│B], and is read 'the probability of A, given B'.

Joint probability is the probability of two events in conjunction. That is, it is the probability of both events together. The joint probability of A and B is written $P(A \cap B)$ or $P(A,B)$.

a. Quantile
b. Sample space
c. Renewal theory
d. Conditional probability

25. _____ is the mathematical operation of scaling one number by another. It is one of the four basic operations in elementary arithmetic.

_____ is defined for whole numbers in terms of repeated addition; for example, 4 multiplied by 3 can be calculated by adding 3 copies of 4 together:

$$4 + 4 + 4 = 12.$$

_____ of rational numbers and real numbers is defined by systematic generalization of this basic idea.

a. The number 0 is even.
b. Highest common factor
c. Least common multiple
d. Multiplication

26. In mathematics, a _____ is a rectangular table of elements, which may be numbers or, more generally, any abstract quantities that can be added and multiplied. Matrices are used to describe linear equations, keep track of the coefficients of linear transformations and to record data that depend on multiple parameters. Matrices are described by the field of _____ theory.

a. Double counting
b. Compression
c. Coherent
d. Matrix

27. In mathematics, a stochastic matrix, probability matrix, or _____ is used to describe the transitions of a Markov chain. It has found use in probability theory, statistics and linear algebra, as well as computer science. There are several different definitions and types of stochastic matrices;

   A right stochastic matrix is a square matrix each of whose rows consists of nonnegative real numbers, with each row summing to 1.

a. Sylvester matrix
b. Transition matrix
c. Pick matrix
d. Hessenberg matrix

28. In mathematics, a _____, named after Andrey Markov, is a stochastic process with the Markov property. Having the Markov property means that, given the present state, future states are independent of the past states. In other words, the description of the present state fully captures all the information that could influence the future evolution of the process. Future states will be reached through a probabilistic process instead of a deterministic one.

Chapter 7. PROBABILITY 57

a. Variance-to-mean ratio
b. Possibility theory
c. Law of Truly Large Numbers
d. Markov chain

29.   A _____, named after the Russian mathematician Andrey Markov, is a mathematical model for the random evolution of a memoryless system, that is, one for which the likelihood of a given future state, at any given moment, depends only on its present state, and not on any past states.

In a common description, a stochastic process with the Markov property, or memorylessness, is one for which conditional on the present state of the system, its future and past are independent.

Often, the term Markov chain is used to mean a discrete-time _____.

a. Polar distribution
b. Markov process
c. Random measure
d. Hellinger distance

Chapter 8. STATISTICS

1. _____ are used to describe the basic features of the data gathered from an experimental study in various ways. A _____ is distinguished from inductive statistics. They provide simple summaries about the sample and the measures.
   a. Null hypothesis
   b. Biostatistics
   c. Failure rate
   d. Descriptive statistics

2. A _____ is the result of applying a function to a set of data.

More formally, statistical theory defines a _____ as a function of a sample where the function itself is independent of the sample's distribution: the term is used both for the function and for the value of the function on a given sample.

A _____ is distinct from an unknown statistical parameter, which is not computable from a sample.

   a. Spatial dependence
   b. Statistic
   c. Parameter space
   d. Loss function

3. _____ is a mathematical science pertaining to the collection, analysis, interpretation or explanation, and presentation of data. It also provides tools for prediction and forecasting based on data. It is applicable to a wide variety of academic disciplines, from the natural and social sciences to the humanities, government and business.
   a. Probability distribution
   b. Percentile rank
   c. Regression toward the mean
   d. Statistics

4. In statistics the _____ of an event i is the number n_i of times the event occurred in the experiment or the study. These frequencies are often graphically represented in histograms.

We speak of absolute frequencies, when the counts n_i themselves are given and of

$$f_i = \frac{n_i}{N} = \frac{n_i}{\sum_i n_i}$$

Taking the f_i for all i and tabulating or plotting them leads to a _____ distribution.

a. Frequency
b. Subharmonic
c. Digital room correction
d. Robinson-Dadson curves

5. The term qualitative is used to describe certain types of information. _____ are described in terms of quality. This is the converse of quantitative, which more precisely describes data in terms of quantity and often using a numerical figure to represent something in a statement.
    a. Level of measurement
    b. Missing values
    c. Qualitative data
    d. Nominal category

6. In differential geometry, a discipline within mathematics, a _____ is a subset of the tangent bundle of a manifold satisfying certain properties. _____s are used to build up notions of integrability, and specifically of a foliation of a manifold
    a. Distribution
    b. Discontinuity
    c. Constraint
    d. Coherence

7. In botany, a _____ is an above-ground plant organ specialized for photosynthesis. For this purpose, a _____ is typically flat and thin, to expose the cells containing chloroplast to light over a broad area, and to allow light to penetrate fully into the tissues. Leaves are also the sites in most plants where transpiration and guttation take place.
    a. 120-cell
    b. Leaf
    c. 2-3 heap
    d. 1-center problem

8. A _____ is is a graphical technique for presenting a data set drawn by hand or produced by a mechanical or electronic plotter. It is a graph depicting the relationship between two or more variables used, for instance, in visualising scientific data.

_____s play an important role in statistics and data analysis.

a. Plot
b. C-35
c. Lattice
d. Dini

9. In probability theory, a probability distribution is called _____ if its cumulative distribution function is _____. That is equivalent to saying that for random variables X with the distribution in question, Pr[X = a] = 0 for all real numbers a. If the distribution of X is _____ then X is called a _____ random variable.

a. Conull set
b. Concatenated codes
c. Continuous phase modulation
d. Continuous

10. In statistics, a _____ is a graphical display of tabulated frequencies, shown as bars. It shows what proportion of cases fall into each of several categories. A _____ differs from a bar chart in that it is the area of the bar that denotes the value, not the height as in bar charts, a crucial distinction when the categories are not of uniform width.

a. Standardized moment
b. First-hitting-time models
c. Histogram
d. Probability distribution

11. A _____ is a circular chart divided into sectors, illustrating relative magnitudes or frequences or percents. In a _____, the arc length of each sector, is proportional to the quantity it represents. Together, the sectors create a full disk.

a. 1-center problem
b. 2-3 heap
c. 120-cell
d. Pie chart

12. In mathematics, an _____, or central tendency of a data set refers to a measure of the 'middle' or 'expected' value of the data set. There are many different descriptive statistics that can be chosen as a measurement of the central tendency of the data items.

An _____ is a single value that is meant to typify a list of values.

a. Average
b. A posteriori
c. A chemical equation
d. A Mathematical Theory of Communication

13. In mathematics, an average, or _____ of a data set refers to a measure of the 'middle' or 'expected' value of the data set. There are many different descriptive statistics that can be chosen as a measurement of the _____ of the data items.

An average is a single value that is meant to typify a list of values.

a. Central tendency
b. Trimean
c. Quartile
d. Mean reciprocal rank

14. In statistics, _____ has two related meanings:

- the arithmetic _____.
- the expected value of a random variable, which is also called the population _____.

It is sometimes stated that the '_____' _____s average. This is incorrect if '_____' is taken in the specific sense of 'arithmetic _____' as there are different types of averages: the _____, median, and mode. For instance, average house prices almost always use the median value for the average.

For a real-valued random variable X, the _____ is the expectation of X.

a. Proportional hazards model
b. Mean
c. Probability
d. Statistical population

15. In mathematics the concept of a _____ generalizes notions such as 'length', 'area', and 'volume'. Informally, given some base set, a '_____' is any consistent assignment of 'sizes' to the subsets of the base set. Depending on the application, the 'size' of a subset may be interpreted as its physical size, the amount of something that lies within the subset, or the probability that some random process will yield a result within the subset.

a. Cusp
b. Lattice
c. Measure
d. Congruent

16. In statistics, a _____ is a subset of a population. Typically, the population is very large, making a census or a complete enumeration of all the values in the population impractical or impossible. The _____ represents a subset of manageable size.

 a. Duality
 b. Boussinesq approximation
 c. Dispersion
 d. Sample

17. In statistics, a _____ is a list of the values that a variable takes in a sample. It is usually a list, ordered by quantity, showing the number of times each value appears. For example, if 100 people rate a five-point Likert scale assessing their agreement with a statement on a scale on which 1 denotes strong agreement and 5 strong disagreement, the _____ of their responses might look like:

This simple tabulation has two drawbacks.

 a. Percentile
 b. Confounding
 c. Covariance
 d. Frequency distribution

18. In geometry, a _____ of a triangle is a line segment joining a vertex to the midpoint of the opposing side. Every triangle has exactly three _____s; one running from each vertex to the opposite side.

The three _____s are concurrent at a point known as the triangle's centroid, or center of mass of the triangle.

 a. Median
 b. Percentile rank
 c. Statistical significance
 d. Correlation

Chapter 8. STATISTICS

19. In statistics, the _____ is the value that occurs the most frequently in a data set or a probability distribution. In some fields, notably education, sample data are often called scores, and the sample _____ is known as the modal score.

Like the statistical mean and the median, the _____ is a way of capturing important information about a random variable or a population in a single quantity.

 a. Field
 b. Function
 c. Deltoid
 d. Mode

20. In probability theory, an _____ is a set of outcomes to which a probability is assigned. Typically, when the sample space is finite, any subset of the sample space is an _____. However, this approach does not work well in cases where the sample space is infinite, most notably when the outcome is a real number.
 a. Audio compression
 b. Equaliser
 c. Information set
 d. Event

21. In mathematics, the _____ of two sets A and B is the set that contains all elements of A that also belong to B, but no other elements.

For explanation of the symbols used in this article, refer to the table of mathematical symbols.

The _____ of A and B

The _____ of A and B is written 'A ∩ B'. Formally:

> x is an element of A ∩ B if and only if
> - x is an element of A and
> - x is an element of B.
>
> For example:
> - The _____ of the sets {1, 2, 3} and {2, 3, 4} is {2, 3}.
> - The number 9 is not in the _____ of the set of prime numbers {2, 3, 5, 7, 11, â€¦} and the set of odd numbers {1, 3, 5, 7, 9, 11, â€¦}.

If the _____ of two sets A and B is empty, that is they have no elements in common, then they are said to be disjoint, denoted: A ∩ B = Ø. For example the sets {1, 2} and {3, 4} are disjoint, written
{1, 2} ∩ {3, 4} = Ø.

a. Order
b. Erlang
c. Intersection
d. Advice

22. In optics, _____ is the phenomenon in which the phase velocity of a wave depends on its frequency. Media having such a property are termed dispersive media.

The most familiar example of _____ is probably a rainbow, in which _____ causes the spatial separation of a white light into components of different wavelengths.

a. Boussinesq approximation
b. Dispersion
c. Crib
d. Depth

23. In descriptive statistics, the _____ is the length of the smallest interval which contains all the data. It is calculated by subtracting the smallest observations from the greatest and provides an indication of statistical dispersion.

It is measured in the same units as the data.

a. Bandwidth
b. Class
c. Kernel
d. Range

24. In mathematics and statistics, _____ is a measure of difference for interval and ratio variables between the observed value and the mean. The sign of _____, either positive or negative, indicates whether the observation is larger than or smaller than the mean. The magnitude of the value reports how different an observation is from the mean.
a. Deviation
b. Filter
c. Conchoid
d. Functional

25. In probability and statistics, the _____ is a measure of the dispersion of a collection of numbers. It can apply to a probability distribution, a random variable, a population or a data set. The _____ is usually denoted with the letter σ.

Chapter 8. STATISTICS

a. Statistical population
b. Failure rate
c. Null hypothesis
d. Standard deviation

26. In probability theory and statistics, the _____ of a random variable, probability distribution averaging the squared distance of its possible values from the expected value. Whereas the mean is a way to describe the location of a distribution, the _____ is a way to capture its scale or degree of being spread out. The unit of _____ is the square of the unit of the original variable.
    a. Nonlinear regression
    b. Variance
    c. Kendall tau rank correlation coefficient
    d. Probability distribution

27. _____ is usually defined as the activity of using and developing computer technology, computer hardware and software. It is the computer-specific part of information technology. Computer science (or _____ science) is the study and the science of the theoretical foundations of information and computation and their implementation and application in computer systems.
    a. Probabilistic Turing Machine
    b. Deterministic finite state machine
    c. Parallel Random Access Machine
    d. Computing

28. A _____ is the value of a variable below which a certain percent of observations fall. So the 20th _____ is the value below which 20 percent of the observations may be found. The term _____ and the related term _____ rank are often used in descriptive statistics as well as in the reporting of scores from norm-referenced tests.
    a. Percentile
    b. Frequency distribution
    c. Logistic regression
    d. Statistically significant

29. In mathematics, the _____ of an abelian group measures how large a group is in terms of how large a vector space over the rational numbers one would need to 'contain' it; or alternatively how large a free abelian group it can contain as a subgroup.

The _____ of a finite abelian group has a different definition.

An abelian group is often thought of as composed of its torsion subgroup T, and its torsion-free part A/T.

Chapter 8. STATISTICS

a. Discontinuity
b. Chord
c. Coherence
d. Rank

30. The _____ of any solid, plasma, vacuum or theoretical object is how much three-dimensional space it occupies, often quantified numerically. One-dimensional figures and two-dimensional shapes are assigned zero _____ in the three-dimensional space. _____ is presented as ml or cm^3.

_____s of straight-edged and circular shapes are calculated using arithmetic formulae.

a. Volume
b. Cauchy momentum equation
c. Thermodynamic limit
d. Stress-energy tensor

31. _____ is a dimensionless quantity derived by subtracting the population mean from an individual raw score and then dividing the difference by the population standard deviation.

a. 120-cell
b. 1-center problem
c. 2-3 heap
d. Z-score

32. In descriptive statistics, a _____ is a convenient way of graphically depicting the five-number summary, which consists of the smallest observation, lower quartile (Q1), median, upper quartile (Q3), and largest observation; in addition, the _____ indicates which observations, if any, are considered unusual, or outliers.

a. Mathematical model
b. Non-linear least squares
c. Point-slope form
d. Box plot

33. In descriptive statistics, a _____ is any of the three values which divide the sorted data set into four equal parts, so that each part represents one fourth of the sampled population.

- first _____ = lower _____ = cuts off lowest 25% of data = 25th percentile
- second _____ = median = cuts data set in half = 50th percentile
- third _____ = upper _____ = cuts off highest 25% of data, or lowest 75% = 75th percentile

The difference between the upper and lower _____s is called the interquartile range.

There is no universal agreement on choosing the _____ values.

The formula for the position of the observation at a given percentile, y, with n data points sorted in ascending order is:

$$L_y = (n+1)\left(\frac{y}{100}\right)$$

Example 4.
   a. Seven-number summary
   b. Mean reciprocal rank
   c. Trimean
   d. Quartile

34.   In mathematics, a _____ is a statement that can be proved on the basis of explicitly stated or previously agreed assumptions.
   a. Theorem
   b. Logical value
   c. Boolean function
   d. Disjunction introduction

35.   The word _____ denotes information gained by means of observation, experience as opposed to theoretical. A central concept in science and the scientific method is that all evidence must be _____ that is, dependent on evidence or consequences that are observable by the senses. It is usually differentiated from the philosophic usage of empiricism by the use of the adjective '_____' or the adverb 'empirically.' '_____' as an adjective or adverb is used in conjunction with both the natural and social sciences, and refers to the use of working hypotheses that are testable using observation or experiment.
   a. Empirical
   b. A chemical equation
   c. A posteriori
   d. A Mathematical Theory of Communication

36.   _____ or experimental probability, is the ratio of the number favorable outcomes to the total number of trials , not in a sample space but in an actual sequence of experiments. In a more general sense, _____ estimates probabilities from experience and observation. The phrase a posteriori probability has also been used an alternative to _____ or relative frequency.

Chapter 8. STATISTICS

a. A Mathematical Theory of Communication
b. A posteriori
c. A chemical equation
d. Empirical probability

37. _____ is the likelihood or chance that something is the case or will happen. Theoretical _____ is used extensively in areas such as statistics, mathematics, science and philosophy to draw conclusions about the likelihood of potential events and the underlying mechanics of complex systems.

The word _____ does not have a consistent direct definition.

a. Statistical significance
b. Discrete random variable
c. Standardized moment
d. Probability

38. In mathematics, _____ are used in the study of chance and probability. They were developed to assist in the analysis of games of chance, stochastic events, and the results of scientific experiments by capturing only the mathematical properties necessary to answer probabilistic questions. Further formalizations have firmly grounded the entity in the theoretical domains of mathematics by making use of measure theory.

a. Random variables
b. Statistical dispersion
c. Median polish
d. Statistics

39. In probability theory and statistics, a _____ identifies either the probability of each value of an unidentified random variable, or the probability of the value falling within a particular interval. The probability function describes the range of possible values that a random variable can attain and the probability that the value of the random variable is within any subset of that range.

When the random variable takes values in the set of real numbers, the _____ is completely described by the cumulative distribution function, whose value at each real x is the probability that the random variable is smaller than or equal to x.

a. Z-test
b. Probability distribution
c. Statistical graphics
d. Normal distribution

Chapter 8. STATISTICS

40. In mathematics, an _____ is a statement about the relative size or order of two objects, or about whether they are the same or not

- The notation a < b means that a is less than b.
- The notation a > b means that a is greater than b.
- The notation a ≠ b means that a is not equal to b, but does not say that one is bigger than the other or even that they can be compared in size.

In all these cases, a is not equal to b, hence, '_____'.

These relations are known as strict _____

- The notation a ≤ b means that a is less than or equal to b;
- The notation a ≥ b means that a is greater than or equal to b;

An additional use of the notation is to show that one quantity is much greater than another, normally by several orders of magnitude.

- The notation a << b means that a is much less than b.
- The notation a >> b means that a is much greater than b.

If the sense of the _____ is the same for all values of the variables for which its members are defined, then the _____ is called an 'absolute' or 'unconditional' _____. If the sense of an _____ holds only for certain values of the variables involved, but is reversed or destroyed for other values of the variables, it is called a conditional _____.

An _____ may appear unsolvable because it only states whether a number is larger or smaller than another number; but it is possible to apply the same operations for equalities to inequalities. For example, to find x for the _____ 10x > 23 one would divide 23 by 10.

a. A posteriori
b. A Mathematical Theory of Communication
c. A chemical equation
d. Inequality

41. In mathematics a _____ is an inequality which involves a linear function.

When operating in terms of real numbers, linear inequalities are the ones written in the forms

$$f(x) < b \text{ or } f(x) \leq b,$$

where f(x) is a linear functional in real numbers and b is a constant real number. Alternatively, these may be viewed as

$$g(x) < 0 \text{ or } g(x) \leq 0,$$

where g(x) is an affine function.

a. Linear inequality
b. Levi-Civita symbol
c. Split-complex number
d. Generalized singular value decomposition

42. In probability theory and statistics, the _____ of a random variable is the integral of the random variable with respect to its probability measure. For discrete random variables this is equivalent to the probability-weighted sum of the possible values, and for continuous random variables with a density function it is the probability density -weighted integral of the possible values.

The _____ may be intuitively understood by the law of large numbers: The _____, when it exists, is almost surely the limit of the sample mean as sample size grows to infinity.

a. Illustration
b. Infinitely divisible distribution
c. Expected value
d. Event

43. In elementary algebra, a _____ is a polynomial with two terms: the sum of two monomials. It is the simplest kind of polynomial except for a monomial.

The _____ a² - b² can be factored as the product of two other _____s:

a² - b² .

The product of a pair of linear _____s a x + b and c x + d is:

2 +x + bd.

Chapter 8. STATISTICS

A _____ raised to the nth power, represented as

n

can be expanded by means of the _____ theorem or, equivalently, using Pascal's triangle.

   a. Rational root theorem
   b. Binomial
   c. Real structure
   d. Cylindrical algebraic decomposition

44. In scientific inquiry, an _____ is a method of investigating particular types of research questions or solving particular types of problems. The _____ is a cornerstone in the empirical approach to acquiring deeper knowledge about the world and is used in both natural sciences as well as in social sciences. An _____ is defined, in science, as a method of investigating less known fields, solving practical problems and proving theoretical assumptions.
   a. A Mathematical Theory of Communication
   b. A posteriori
   c. Experiment
   d. A chemical equation

45. In game theory, an _____ is a set of moves or strategies taken by the players, or their payoffs resulting from the actions or strategies taken by all players. The two are complementary in that given knowledge of the set of strategies of all players, the final state of the game is known, as are any relevant payoffs. In a game where chance or a random event is involved, the _____ is not known from only the set of strategies, but is only realized when the random even are realized.
   a. Outcome
   b. Equaliser
   c. Autonomous system
   d. Algebraic

46. _____ typically deals with the probability of several successive decisions, each of which has two possible outcomes.

The probability of an event can be expressed as a _____ if its outcomes can be broken down into two probabilities p and q, where p and q are complementary For example, tossing a coin can be either heads or tails, each which have a probability of 0.5. Rolling a four on a six-sided die can be expressed as the probability of getting a 4 or the probability of rolling something else.

a. Quantile
b. Binomial Probability
c. Markov chain
d. Marginal distribution

47. In probability theory and statistics, the _____ is the discrete probability distribution of the number of successes in a sequence of n independent yes/no experiments, each of which yields success with probability p. Such a success/failure experiment is also called a Bernoulli experiment or Bernoulli trial. In fact, when n = 1, the _____ is a Bernoulli distribution.
  a. Binomial distribution
  b. Biostatistics
  c. Coefficient of variation
  d. Median

48. In mathematics, specifically in combinatorial commutative algebra, a convex lattice polytope P is called _____ if it has the following property: given any positive integer n, every lattice point of the dilation nP, obtained from P by scaling its vertices by the factor n and taking the convex hull of the resulting points, can be written as the sum of exactly n lattice points in P. This property plays an important role in the theory of toric varieties, where it corresponds to projective normality of the toric variety determined by P.

The simplex in R^k with the vertices at the origin and along the unit coordinate vectors is _____.

  a. Polytetrahedron
  b. Normal
  c. Hypercube
  d. Demihypercubes

49. In mathematics, the concept of a _____ tries to capture the intuitive idea of a geometrical one-dimensional and continuous object. A simple example is the circle. In everyday use of the term '_____', a straight line is not curved, but in mathematical parlance _____s include straight lines and line segments.
  a. Kappa curve
  b. Curve
  c. Quadrifolium
  d. Negative pedal curve

Chapter 8. STATISTICS

50. _____ is a quantity expressing the two-dimensional size of a defined part of a surface, typically a region bounded by a closed curve. The term surface _____ refers to the total _____ of the exposed surface of a 3-dimensional solid, such as the sum of the _____s of the exposed sides of a polyhedron. _____ is an important invariant in the differential geometry of surfaces.
   a. A posteriori
   b. A chemical equation
   c. A Mathematical Theory of Communication
   d. Area

51. The _____ is an important family of continuous probability distributions, applicable in many fields. Each member of the family may be defined by two parameters, location and scale: the mean and variance respectively. The standard _____ is the _____ with a mean of zero and a variance of one.
   a. Coefficient of variation
   b. Percentile rank
   c. Normal distribution
   d. Null hypothesis

52. A _____ also called the 'Unit Normal Table' is a table that is used to find the probability that a statistic is observed below, above and by extension, any normal distribution.

Normal distributions are symmetrical, bell-shaped distributions that are useful in describing real-world data. The standard normal distribution, represented by the letter Z, is the normal distribution having a mean of 0 and a standard deviation of 1.

   a. Standard normal table
   b. Skew normal distribution
   c. Nakagami distribution
   d. Gumbel distribution

53. _____ is a special mathematical relationship between two quantities. Two quantities are called proportional if they vary in such a way that one of the quantities is a constant multiple of the other, or equivalently if they have a constant ratio.
   a. Depth
   b. Discontinuity
   c. Proportionality
   d. Compression

Chapter 8. STATISTICS

54. Following a statistical study, a layman may well ask: 'How much _____ can we have in these conclusions?'. A problem immediately arises because a statistician's technical understanding of the term '_____' can differ radically from a layperson's.

The question 'how much _____ can we have in these conclusions?' can have several ramifications, some of which are:

- how reliable are the individual items of data being analysed: do the values measure what they are supposed to measure?
- how extensive is the dataset?
- how representative of the target population is the sample selected?
- how accurately can the important quantities be estimated from the dataset?
- if testing that an intervention has an effect, what is the smallest size of effect that could reliably have been detected from such a dataset as was available.

The last two questions correspond broadly to outcomes of statistical analyses using _____ intervals and examining the statistical power of a test, but careful interpretation is needed. Other statistical approches to these questions are available.

a. 2-3 heap
b. 1-center problem
c. Confidence
d. 120-cell

55. In statistics, a _____ or confidence bound is an interval estimate of a population parameter. Instead of estimating the parameter by a single value, an interval likely to include the parameter is given. Thus, _____s are used to indicate the reliability of an estimate.
a. Time series
b. Kurtosis
c. Percentile rank
d. Confidence interval

56. In mathematics, a _____ is a set of real numbers with the property that any number that lies between two numbers in the set is also included in the set. For example, the set of all numbers x satisfying $0 \leq x \leq 1$ is an _____ which contains 0 and 1, as well as all numbers between them. Other examples of _____s are the set of all real numbers $\mathbb{R}$, the set of all positive real numbers, and the empty set.

a. Ideal
b. Order
c. Interval
d. Annihilator

57. The _____ of a method of measurement or estimation is the estimated standard deviation of the error in that method. Specifically, it estimates the standard deviation of the difference between the measured or estimated values and the true values. Notice that the true value of the standard deviation is usually unknown and the use of the term _____ carries with it the idea that an estimate of this unknown quantity is being used.

a. Chiral
b. Dini
c. Center
d. Standard error

58. The _____ states that the re-averaged sum of a sufficiently large number of identically distributed independent random variables each with finite mean and variance will be approximately normally distributed . *Formally, a _____ is any of a set of weak-convergence results in probability theory. They all express the fact that any sum of many independent identically distributed random variables will tend to be distributed according to a particular 'attractor distribution'.*

a. Regular conditional probability
b. Probability interpretations
c. Central Limit Theorem
d. Conditional probability

59. In mathematics, the concept of a '_____' is used to describe the behavior of a function as its argument or input either 'gets close' to some point, or as the argument becomes arbitrarily large; or the behavior of a sequence's elements as their index increases indefinitely. _____s are used in calculus and other branches of mathematical analysis to define derivatives and continuity.

In formulas, _____ is usually abbreviated as lim.

a. Copula
b. Contact
c. Duality
d. Limit

76   *Chapter 9. GAME THEORY*

1. A _____ is a structured activity, usually undertaken for enjoyment and sometimes also used as an educational tool. _____s are distinct from work, which is usually carried out for remuneration, and from art, which is more concerned with the expression of ideas. However, the distinction is not clear-cut, and many _____s are also considered to be work (such as professional players of spectator sports/_____s) or art (such as jigsaw puzzles or _____s involving an artistic layout such as Mah-jongg solitaire.)
   a. 120-cell
   b. 1-center problem
   c. 2-3 heap
   d. Game

2. In mathematics, a _____ is a rectangular table of elements, which may be numbers or, more generally, any abstract quantities that can be added and multiplied. Matrices are used to describe linear equations, keep track of the coefficients of linear transformations and to record data that depend on multiple parameters. Matrices are described by the field of _____ theory.
   a. Compression
   b. Coherent
   c. Double counting
   d. Matrix

3. In game theory, a player's _____ in a game is a complete plan of action for whatever situation might arise; this fully determines the player's behaviour. A player's _____ will determine the action the player will take at any stage of the game, for every possible history of play up to that stage.

A _____ profile is a set of strategies for each player which fully specifies all actions in a game.

   a. Correlated equilibrium
   b. Matching pennies
   c. Sir Philip Sidney game
   d. Strategy

4. In mathematics, a _____ is a point in the domain of a function of two variables which is a stationary point but not a local extremum. At such a point, in general, the surface resembles a saddle that curves up in one direction, and curves down in a different direction. In terms of contour lines, a _____ can be recognized, in general, by a contour that appears to intersect itself.
   a. 1-center problem
   b. Gauss-Codazzi equations
   c. Gauss map
   d. Saddle point

Chapter 9. GAME THEORY

5. _____ is the likelihood or chance that something is the case or will happen. Theoretical _____ is used extensively in areas such as statistics, mathematics, science and philosophy to draw conclusions about the likelihood of potential events and the underlying mechanics of complex systems.

The word _____ does not have a consistent direct definition.

a. Discrete random variable
b. Probability
c. Standardized moment
d. Statistical significance

6. In decision theory, a decision rule is said to _____ another if the performance of the former is sometimes better, and never worse, than that of the latter.

Formally, let δ_1 and δ_2 be two decision rules, and let R be the risk of rule δ for parameter θ. The decision rule δ_1 is said to _____ the rule δ_2 if $R(\theta, \delta_1) \leq R(\theta, \delta_2)$ for all θ, and the inequality is strict for some θ.

a. Dominate
b. Freedman-Diaconis rule
c. Pivotal quantity
d. Higher-order statistics

Chapter 10. LOGIC

1. _____ is the study of the principles of valid demonstration and inference. _____ is a branch of philosophy, a part of the classical trivium of grammar, _____, and rhetoric. of λογικῖŒς, 'possessed of reason, intellectual, dialectical, argumentative', from λῖŒγος logos, 'word, thought, idea, argument, account, reason, or principle'.
   a. Logic
   b. Satisfiability
   c. Counterpart theory
   d. Boolean function

2. A _____ is a mathematical table used in logic -- specifically in connection with Boolean algebra, boolean functions, and propositional calculus -- to compute the functional values of logical expressions on each of their functional arguments, that is, on each combination of values taken by their logical variables. In particular, _____s can be used to tell whether a propositional expression is true for all legitimate input values, that is, logically valid.

   The pattern of reasoning that the _____ tabulates was Frege's, Peirce's, and Schröder's by 1880.

   a. 1-center problem
   b. 2-3 heap
   c. 120-cell
   d. Truth table

3. In logic and mathematics, or, also known as logical _____ or inclusive _____ is a logical operator that results in true whenever one or more of its operands are true. In grammar, or is a coordinating conjunction. In ordinary language 'or' rather has the meaning of exclusive _____.
   a. Triquetra
   b. Cube
   c. Zero-point energy
   d. Disjunction

4. An _____ is one that cannot be compressed because it lacks sufficient repeating sequences. Whether a string is compressible will often depend on the algorithm being used. Some examples may illuminate this.
   a. Entropy encoding
   b. Incompressible string
   c. A Mathematical Theory of Communication
   d. Arithmetic coding

5. In logic and mathematics, _____ or not is an operation on logical values, for example, the logical value of a proposition, that sends true to false and false to true. Intuitively, the _____ of a proposition holds exactly when that proposition does not hold. In grammar, nor is an adverb which acts as a coordinating conjunction.

a. Syntax
b. Sentence diagram
c. 1-center problem
d. Negation

6. In propositional logic, contraposition is a logical relationship between two statements of material implication. A proposition Q is materially implicated by a proposition P when the following relationship holds:

$$(P \rightarrow Q)$$

In vernacular terms, this states 'If P then Q', or, 'If Socrates is a man then Socrates is human.' In a conditional such as this, P is called the antecedent and Q the consequent. One statement is the _____ of the other just when its antecedent is the negated consequent of the other, and vice-versa.

a. Control chart
b. Contour map
c. Contrapositive
d. Continuous signal

7. In the study of metric spaces in mathematics, there are various notions of two metrics on the same underlying space being 'the same', or _____.

In the following, M will denote a non-empty set and d_1 and d_2 will denote two metrics on M.

The two metrics d_1 and d_2 are said to be topologically _____ if they generate the same topology on M.

a. A posteriori
b. A Mathematical Theory of Communication
c. A chemical equation
d. Equivalent

8. In mathematics, a _____ is a convincing demonstration that some mathematical statement is necessarily true. _____s are obtained from deductive reasoning, rather than from inductive or empirical arguments. That is, a _____ must demonstrate that a statement is true in all cases, without a single exception.

a. Germ
b. Congruent
c. Conchoid
d. Proof

9. The _____ are the set of numbers consisting of the natural numbers including 0 and their negatives. They are numbers that can be written without a fractional or decimal component, and fall within the set {... −2, −1, 0, 1, 2, ...}.
   a. Integers
   b. A posteriori
   c. A Mathematical Theory of Communication
   d. A chemical equation

10. In mathematics, a _____ can mean either an element of the set {1, 2, 3, ...} or an element of the set {0, 1, 2, 3, ...}. The latter is especially preferred in mathematical logic, set theory, and computer science.

    _____s have two main purposes: they can be used for counting, and they can be used for ordering.

    a. Natural number
    b. Suslin cardinal
    c. Cardinal numbers
    d. Strong partition cardinal

11. The mathematical concept of a _____ expresses the intuitive idea of deterministic dependence between two quantities, one of which is viewed as primary and the other as secondary. A _____ then is a way to associate a unique output for each input of a specified type, for example, a real number or an element of a given set.
    a. Function
    b. Coherent
    c. Grill
    d. Going up

12. In mathematics, a _____ is a picture of a straight line in which the integers are shown as specially-marked points evenly spaced on the line. Although this image only shows the integers from -9 to 9, the line includes all real numbers, continuing 'forever' in each direction. It is often used as an aid in teaching simple addition and subtraction, especially involving negative numbers.

Chapter 10. LOGIC

a. Number system
b. Number Line
c. Real number
d. Point plotting

13. In mathematics, a _____ is a number which can be expressed as a ratio of two integers. Non-integer _____s are usually written as the vulgar fraction $\frac{a}{b}$, where b is not zero. a is called the numerator, and b the denominator.

a. Rational number
b. Pre-algebra
c. Minkowski distance
d. Tally marks

14. In mathematics, the _____s may be described informally in several different ways. The _____s include both rational numbers, such as 42 and −23/129, and irrational numbers, such as pi and the square root of two; or, a _____ can be given by an infinite decimal representation, such as 2.4871773339...., where the digits continue in some way; or, the _____s may be thought of as points on an infinitely long number line.

These descriptions of the _____s, while intuitively accessible, are not sufficiently rigorous for the purposes of pure mathematics.

a. Minkowski distance
b. Real number
c. Pre-algebra
d. Tally marks

15. A _____ is an algebraic equation in which each term is either a constant or the product of a constant and a single variable. _____s can have one, two, three or more variables.

_____s occur with great regularity in applied mathematics.

a. Linear equation
b. Difference of two squares
c. Quartic equation
d. Quadratic equation

16. In mathematics, a _____ is a rectangular table of elements, which may be numbers or, more generally, any abstract quantities that can be added and multiplied. Matrices are used to describe linear equations, keep track of the coefficients of linear transformations and to record data that depend on multiple parameters. Matrices are described by the field of _____ theory.
   a. Compression
   b. Coherent
   c. Matrix
   d. Double counting

17. The x-axis is the horizontal axis of a two- dimensional plot in the _____, that is typically pointed to the right. Also known as a right-handed coordinate system.
   a. 2-3 heap
   b. 1-center problem
   c. Cartesian coordinate system
   d. 120-cell

18. In mathematics, the _____ of a Euclidean space is a special point, usually denoted by the letter O, used as a fixed point of reference for the geometry of the surrounding space. In a Cartesian coordinate system, the _____ is the point where the axes of the system intersect. In Euclidean geometry, the _____ may be chosen freely as any convenient point of reference.
   a. Autonomous system
   b. Interval
   c. OMAC
   d. Origin

19. The _____ of any solid, plasma, vacuum or theoretical object is how much three-dimensional space it occupies, often quantified numerically. One-dimensional figures and two-dimensional shapes are assigned zero _____ in the three-dimensional space. _____ is presented as ml or cm^3.

   _____s of straight-edged and circular shapes are calculated using arithmetic formulae.

   a. Thermodynamic limit
   b. Volume
   c. Cauchy momentum equation
   d. Stress-energy tensor

20. The _____ is the horizontal axis of a two- dimensional plot in the Cartesian coordinate system, that is typically pointed to the right. Also known as a right-handed coordinate system.

a. X-axis
b. 2-3 heap
c. 1-center problem
d. 120-cell

21. The _____ is one of the coordinates of a point in a two or three-dimensional cartesian coordinate system, equal to the distance of a point from the y-axis in a 2D system, or from the plane of y and z axes in a 3D system, measured along a line parallel to the x axis.
   a. X-coordinate
   b. 1-center problem
   c. 2-3 heap
   d. 120-cell

22. In reference to a 2D and 3D plane, the _____ is the vertical height of a 2D or 3D object.
   a. Y-axis
   b. 1-center problem
   c. 120-cell
   d. 2-3 heap

23. The _____ is the distance between a point and an axis in the Cartesian Coordinate System.
   a. 1-center problem
   b. Y-coordinate
   c. 2-3 heap
   d. 120-cell

24. A _____ consists of one quarter of the coordinate plane.
   a. 2-3 heap
   b. 120-cell
   c. 1-center problem
   d. Quadrant

Chapter 10. LOGIC

25. In mathematics, an _____ is a statement about the relative size or order of two objects, or about whether they are the same or not

- The notation a < b means that a is less than b.
- The notation a > b means that a is greater than b.
- The notation a ≠ b means that a is not equal to b, but does not say that one is bigger than the other or even that they can be compared in size.

In all these cases, a is not equal to b, hence, '_____'.

These relations are known as strict _____

- The notation a ≤ b means that a is less than or equal to b;
- The notation a ≥ b means that a is greater than or equal to b;

An additional use of the notation is to show that one quantity is much greater than another, normally by several orders of magnitude.

- The notation a << b means that a is much less than b.
- The notation a >> b means that a is much greater than b.

If the sense of the _____ is the same for all values of the variables for which its members are defined, then the _____ is called an 'absolute' or 'unconditional' _____. If the sense of an _____ holds only for certain values of the variables involved, but is reversed or destroyed for other values of the variables, it is called a conditional _____.

An _____ may appear unsolvable because it only states whether a number is larger or smaller than another number; but it is possible to apply the same operations for equalities to inequalities. For example, to find x for the _____ 10x > 23 one would divide 23 by 10.

a. A chemical equation
b. A Mathematical Theory of Communication
c. A posteriori
d. Inequality

26. In mathematics, a _____ is a set of real numbers with the property that any number that lies between two numbers in the set is also included in the set. For example, the set of all numbers x satisfying $0 \leq x \leq 1$ is an _____ which contains 0 and 1, as well as all numbers between them. Other examples of _____s are the set of all real numbers $\mathbb{R}$, the set of all positive real numbers, and the empty set.

a. Annihilator
b. Order
c. Ideal
d. Interval

27. _____ is the notation in which permitted values for a variable are expressed as ranging over a certain interval; "5 < x < 9" is an example of the application of _____.
a. A Mathematical Theory of Communication
b. Infinity
c. Interval notation
d. Implicit differentiation

ANSWER KEY

Chapter 1
1. a 2. c 3. c 4. d 5. a 6. d 7. d 8. d 9. d 10. d
11. c 12. d 13. d 14. c 15. d 16. a 17. d 18. c 19. d 20. d
21. b

Chapter 2
1. b 2. d 3. b 4. d 5. b 6. c 7. d 8. a 9. d 10. d
11. c 12. d 13. d 14. d 15. b 16. d 17. b 18. d 19. d 20. a
21. d 22. d 23. a 24. d 25. d 26. c 27. c 28. d 29. d 30. d
31. d 32. d 33. d

Chapter 3
1. d 2. a 3. c 4. c 5. b 6. d 7. d 8. a 9. a 10. d
11. d 12. d 13. a 14. d 15. d 16. c

Chapter 4
1. b 2. a 3. d 4. c 5. b 6. b 7. d 8. c 9. b 10. d
11. c 12. d 13. a 14. d 15. d 16. b

Chapter 5
1. a 2. d 3. d 4. a 5. d 6. a 7. d 8. a 9. d 10. c
11. d

Chapter 6
1. c 2. d 3. b 4. c 5. d 6. a 7. b 8. a 9. d 10. c
11. a 12. b 13. b 14. b 15. b 16. d 17. d 18. d 19. a 20. a
21. d 22. d 23. d 24. d 25. d 26. d 27. d 28. b

Chapter 7
1. d 2. d 3. a 4. c 5. c 6. d 7. a 8. a 9. b 10. d
11. a 12. b 13. c 14. d 15. d 16. d 17. d 18. d 19. d 20. d
21. d 22. d 23. d 24. d 25. d 26. d 27. b 28. d 29. b

Chapter 8
1. d 2. b 3. d 4. a 5. c 6. a 7. b 8. a 9. d 10. c
11. d 12. a 13. a 14. b 15. c 16. d 17. d 18. a 19. d 20. d
21. c 22. b 23. d 24. a 25. d 26. b 27. d 28. a 29. d 30. a
31. d 32. d 33. d 34. a 35. a 36. d 37. d 38. a 39. b 40. d
41. a 42. c 43. b 44. c 45. a 46. b 47. a 48. b 49. b 50. d
51. c 52. a 53. c 54. c 55. d 56. c 57. d 58. c 59. d

Chapter 9
1. d 2. d 3. d 4. d 5. b 6. a

ANSWER KEY

Chapter 10

1. a	2. d	3. d	4. b	5. d	6. c	7. d	8. d	9. a	10. a
11. a	12. b	13. a	14. b	15. a	16. c	17. c	18. d	19. b	20. a
21. a	22. a	23. b	24. d	25. d	26. d	27. c			

www.ingramcontent.com/pod-product-compliance
Lightning Source LLC
Chambersburg PA
CBHW081848230426
43669CB00018B/2861